# Gwrthryf[ Uprising

## An anthology of Radical Poetry from Contemporary Wales

### Edited by
### Mike Jenkins

*'... red against the inn,*
*Stained with sweat and the shrieks of women*
*Scuttling, crazy, round the corpses humped*
*Like sodden coalsacks on the streaming stones...'*

—Prof Gwyn A. Williams, 'Castle Cinema, Merthyr'

*'No revolutionary movement is complete without its poetical expression'*
—James Connolly

**Culture Matters Co-Operative Ltd.** promotes a socialist and progressive approach to art, culture and politics. See www.culturematters.org.uk

Text Copyright © the contributors
All images Copyright © Gustavius Payne
Copy edited by Dan Hoy and Mike Jarvie
Layout and typesetting by Alan Morrison
ISBN 978-1-912710-48-5

## Acknowledgements

Thanks to the GMB, Merthyr Trades Council and Left Unity Cymru for their generous backing for this anthology / diolch o galon i'r Undeb GMB, Cyngor Undebau Llafur Merthyr a hefyd Undod Chwith Cymru.

# Contents

Part 3: *Protest*

Part 4: *Crynu / Shiver*

Part 5: *Agorwch eich llygaid / Open your eyes*

# Foreword

*By Peter Jones*

Wales: the Land of Song—or so I was always told as a child in hot Mediterranean climes and cold Germanic winters. And not for a decade would I set foot in the Land of my Fathers, Tir fy nhadau, where, through teenage years, culture and community, and yes, some language, seeped through my pores into my veins, my heart, my soul. To be snatched away in a not-so-foreign neighbouring land until a new millennium was born and then I understood the meaning of 'hiraeth'—nostalgia.

Land of song? Aye, and of poetry, fable, eisteddfodau, dragons, rugby... and rebellion. All of which can be found between these covers.

Here, in this volume, rebellious poets draw from that common history, common culture, and common desire to speak truth to the world, showing that we, the people of Wales, y werin Gymreig, have the fire of dragons in our words.

Through these words the reader is taken from coal mines to political discourse, from coronavirus to historic heroes, from mountains to valleys, through towns, villages and cities. Through these words readers are taken on journeys—real and imagined, and drenched in the history that formed these ancient Cymric hills and valleys and shores and lakes.

Voices from history—voices of history—spoken in 21st century tongues both English and Cymraeg. Words dug from mines, hewn from quarries, herded from hillsides and forged from furnaces—here be dragons.

Here are 21st century bards using the ancient magic of poetry to bring home the fight—the fight against imperialism, against injustice, against discrimination. Not just here in Cymru, but the world over. Why? Because an injury to one is an injury to all / un yn dioddef, pawb yn dioddef.

# Introduction

## By Mike Jenkins

It's interesting how many poems in this anthology have dates in their titles. In one section alone ('Protest') it begins with Peter Thabit Jones's 'The Protest: Welsh Miner, 1926' and ends with Rebecca Lowe's 'Colston, Bristol 2020'.

Perhaps it's indicative of our times: because of the uncertainty of the pandemic and merging of days and months due to lockdowns, we need to fix ourselves, both in the present and historically.

For my own town of Merthyr Tydfil—once the very hub of the Industrial Revolution in the 19th century—one date has so much resonance.

1831 saw the Merthyr Rising, when at least 60 working people were killed by the British Army as they rose up against debt, poverty and the iron rule of the ironmasters at that time, particularly Guest, Crawshay and Bacon.

There is still no memorial to those who died, though there is a plaque for the working-class martyr Dic Penderyn, hung for an attack on a constable he never carried out.

It wasn't always seen as an uprising; even today, in Welsh, the word 'Safiad' (meaning stand or stance) is often used instead of the much more accurate and appropriate 'gwrthryfel', suggesting a rebellion.

The great Marxist historian from Dowlais, Prof Gwyn A. Williams was the one who raised the event from 'Riot' to 'Rising' with his book *The Merthyr Rising*. He elevated it to an extremely significant working-class revolt, where the red flag was proudly flown, perhaps for the very first time.

Words and terms are so vital to our consciousness. The authorities read the Riot Act and their version of history portrayed the people as simply recalcitrant.

The very adoption of the word 'Rising' claims the events for the Welsh-speaking workers of the town itself and 'Gwyn Alf' (as he became affectionately known throughout Cymru) showed how their actions clearly had purpose and many causes.

If there was ever an historical event deserving of an epic film such as Mike Leigh's *Peterloo*, it is definitely this Rising, with its leaders like Lewis Lewis, its martyrs like Dic Penderyn and its many forgotten and nameless victims—not to mention its place in working-class organisation and solidarity, of course.

Will we see other risings like those of Black Lives Matter and Extinction Rebellion, and the Indy movements of Scotland and Cymru, and will they change the nature of the British state forever?

While our streets seem quiet at present, it's surely only a matter of time, and the majority of poems in this anthology testify to the righteous anger felt by many against an unjust system.

There are those who argue that poetry has no place in all this, that it's only for raising questions about the world, not posing solutions.

Yet these poems are surely not didactic, but generally reflect on the realities of oppression on its many levels. For politics is not the narrow confines of parties and elections, but the wider concerns of everyone.

In Cymru specifically, poets feel closer to our history because it has largely been kept from us at school—by a Labour administration, incidentally. It becomes, like our language itself, the discovery of a buried identity: one which, when resurrected, opens our senses to people and places around us. We dive deep into the reservoir to discover ourselves, not to drown in our misery.

# Part 1

# Gwrthryfel / Uprising

# The Apprehending of Richard Lewis of Penderyn

You never saw so wretched a country,
the soil barren, mountainous, fruitful in nothing but iron.
And the air strangely cold,
as if in May it is the midst of winter.

The town has the marks that oppression
and bad government give,
and to add to the little accommodating an army can meet with
in so awful a place, not a soul is seen at hamlet or hillside
but as we come marching,
is flying to declivities,
what shelves in the ground are left by scrapping and scraping
for ore and pit coal,
and to such poor oak woods as still avoid the axe,
in the search for a last stave of char.

We come at last to the spot,
it, at a narrow, blackened, thoroughfare,
an inn called Castle.
We meet them, the roustabouts, the villains, traitors to the King.
Violent enough in weskits and pit-boots,
and strong as oxen,
for all they say in bad tongue, they starve.

They've weapons enough, edges and points.
And we in the struggle have the butts, flats of the blades.
A few swords fall, and they can grasp them.
The volley puts some down,
but in the melee the loose blades come up.
No one sees who, but a point takes the thigh,
up under the skirt,
grating at the-bone, stitching the pure white flesh.

At the Great House, with my master Cosher,
all jurisdiction and mighty importance,
the only seat now of the Royal Government of England,
they come with lanthorns, and blazing torches
lighting their naked steel.

We learn they've taken the baggage train,
the bread and bonnets are theirs, with all else,
the tentage, corn, salt pork, the blessed rum.
A few of our own are to nurse their ears from the cudgels.

All this at the climb by the blind pond.
Grand in mist may be, that red wall of Breknoke,
but not my Lord Reay's Land,
neither the shore of Assynt,
with buck deer, antlers like the burning bush,
herding their brides down from the marble hill.
Oh, we come at them there.
There's siege, and some who've known Ireland or India, in pink,
calling order, so it's more than mutiny.
This, the insurrection, out on the heathen hill,
we to be gazing to gentry pastures,
but for the smoke of the infernal blast,
the heaped burthen of the inclines sending always for more,
where the hammered iron goes down.

Across a whale's back of glittering ash, the streams run red
as a pheasant's eye.
We hold him by the arm, his name is Dic;
they say he'll hang.


*Michael Arnold Williams*

## Er cof am Dic Penderyn

Scarred bodies, wounded spirits, a ravaged people.
  Pot bellies, wine saturated minds, a privileged few.
Misery and strife, heartache and hunger, disease and death.
  'This is your heritage', naked words strike deep into the
  infant's heart.
Prosperity, culture and contentment, good health,
    the trappings of man's oppressors; the
    mottos of the masters.
Subjected and exploited, maimed and demented, suffer or rebel.
    Lest that spirit of life be diffused, 'Safwn yn y bwlch'.
    The torch of youth rekindles the flickering spirit of the werin.
Venerated and educated, adorned and sophisticated, submit or destroy.
The audacity of the illiterate masses.
    'An outrageous threat to the company.
    Call out the militia and away with the rabble'.
The throb of rebellion, the intensity of wrath penetrates ill-nurtured minds.
    Fire scorched hearts pound, pumping scolding hot blood into labour-torn
veins.
    From Dowlais down to Plymouth the trembling earth throbs to the beat
of war.
Built from the blood and sweat of the people, the bastion of Cyfarthfa peers
    down disdainfully on the 'commotion'.
The perpetration of suffering, the invincible iron foundation of wealth.
    The dogs bark the master is disturbed.
    'Bara neu waed', cry the tormented souls of the werin.
    'Behave or be damned', cry the cast-iron voices of the masters.
Doomed to failure and ill-prepared, the poor souls ready to storm the walls
of Jericho.
    The motley band dare to challenge the might of the masters,
    protected by the red coats of the King's men, slouch back behind the
comforting walls of the Castle Hotel.
The mortal crack of musket shot penetrates panic-stricken minds.
    Threatened by the wrath and revenge of the English Law, the flame of

revolt is

    extinguished. The caverns of the mind echo to the sound of the fateful shot which

    produced the first martyr of the working class.


*Malcolm Llywelyn*


*Er cof am / in memory of*
*Safwn yn y bwlch / we will make a stand*
*(g)werin / people, the proletariat*
*Bara Neu Waed / Bread Or Blood*

## Gwrthryfel is our name

They read the Riot Act,
sent for soldiers from over the mountains
those ironmasters who would own us.

In thrall and in debt
they can make us destitute,
send bailiffs to take our belongings.

We have toiled long hours
in rolling mills and furnaces;
thirst like a summer of drought.

What are we supposed to do,
while our families' hunger
burns our paltry coal to ashes?

We have seen our babies taken
by disease thriving in grime of rivers,
as they gaze down from mansions.

*Bara Neu Waed* our banners:
our hapless pikes against
their loaded muskets.

*Gwrthryfel* is our name,
we sing it loud and proud
even as Penderyn is hung.

As I remember the blood
on the streets of our town,
no bandages could dam.

As I recall Lewis and the others
banished like common criminals
from a land they'd never see again.

*Mike Jenkins*

*Bara Neu Waed / Bread or Blood*
*Gwrthryfel / Rebellion*

## Becca

*"And they called her Rebekah"*

That day the clouds
Parted like the Dead Sea,
Across the open skies
That were the fields of lords.

Taxes and tithes were the barriers
Burned by the fires of a different tongue.

Fences became charcoaled ribs
That lost their voice of dominion.
Men in their plaid skirts
And farmers' legs
Concealed a brute kiss for the lords.

Welsh knots hissed curses
As the sinewy fires
Made new rules
And the words of outcast
Burned back into hell.


*Jacqueline Jones*

# What a Riot!

*(Wales, 1839)*

Her hat and her Sunday frock
fitted me to a tee, but she said
"Lay off the corset cariad".
But like a fool I would not listen.
Well they said "Come as women",
and the wife never crossed
our threshold without her corset on.
So I would have felt undressed like
without it on, see.

It was a bit snug to start,
however when I was running
and whooping on the Toll Gate
I was fair dying of breath.
Some of the boys even laughed at me
and them all dressed as ladies.
Ladies with beards and hairy arms.

Never since the beginning of time
had St. Clears seen such a sight.
"A most shameful spectacle! A return
to the days of Sodom and Gomorrah"
said the Carmarthen Journal.
We burnt the gates of our oppressors.
We danced and sang, well they did.
My corset was fair killing me for breath.
None of the other boys wore corsets.
However the Reverend had
his wife's pink pantaloons on,
but they say that's a regular thing.
Still I know better for next time.

So up with Rebecca's Daughters!
Down with the Toll Gates!
Down with the Soldiers!
Down with the Whitland Trust!
But take the wife's advice boys
and keep your hands off the corsets.


*Phil Knight*


*Cariad / love*

# In the Shadow of The Great Strike of Penrhyn

Cold on the picket line
no brazier to keep hands warm
though students offer cups of tea

paying twice over.
We smile at colleagues driving in to work
apologetic

almost,
the word *scab* somehow too violent
too quite what—real?

And when lights go on and someone lectures
to a half empty room
is that murmuring

just the way the wind blows
or the ghosts of those who saved tuppence,
thruppence to build this university

and for whom tuppence,
thruppence became fortune—
enough to keep a family off Traitors' Row.


*Julian Brasington*

# Gwlad

They came for my copper.
They came for my gold.
They came for my lead.
They came for my slate.
They came for my coal.
They came for my water.

And they took it. Took all of it.
And when there is nothing left to take
Who will come?

Will no one come to give, not take?
Will no one come to nurture, not exploit?
Will no one come to cherish, not abuse?
Will no one come to love, not rape?


*Patrick Dobbs*

*Gwlad—nation (specifically Wales here)*

## To my Suffragette

*The first suffragette hunger strikes began in July 1909. Marion Wallace Dunlop was released after three and a half days' fasting. By the end of September of that year forcible feeding of prisoners was introduced. This procedure carried on till the outbreak of the First World War when the WSPU—the Women's Social and Political Union—called for a temporary suspension of militancy and the government granted amnesty to all suffragettes in prison.*

Honey, comfrey and calendula,
arnica, hot beef tea, how can we heal you, make you
strong *enough*, now the Cat's released its Mouse,
you, home to us, to our house, to me?

I wasn't meant to be their mother, but we do our best
without you, muddle through, suffer the jibes,
the sly asides, the jeers. Sometimes my peers
leave the paper open by a cartoon
of an ugly, strident woman
doing ugly, strident things...
or slide a postcard under the door,
so crude, so cruel and so unkind, I must admit
I hide them from our girls.

Poultice, salve and balm. I'd like to shield you, keep you from
all harm. Hard for a man to see his sweetheart
hated and harangued,
mistreated, manhandled...
Harder still to know, to feel and not to see.
For what women do to property,
man does now to womankind.

Yet there's no shame for a man who wreaks havoc,
let's go the dogs of war, kills and maims in name

of country, God or cause. No, he's a hero,
of course, garlanded, with honours, statues, property,
acclaim, applauded in epic poem, in songs
of sword and fame, ennobled so his bravery
carries on from son to son to son,
amply rewarded for Grandpappy's crimes.

But she, maker of fire, destroyer of things made
and owned by man, she's wilful, misguided,
out-of-control, harpy or a whore
or a legion of more hateful names.

*Deeds not words*, the Pankhursts said. *Do not appeal,*
*do not grovel, do not beg. Take courage, join hands,*
*stand beside us, fight with us.*

And have you fought, my angel?! You've changed,
grown firmer in resolve, as your body
weakens still. Let me bind you, soothe and comfort you,
clean your cuts, your weals; though your mind's
a stranger to us. Your face hides silent hurts,
secrets left behind the prison door.
Yes, Holloway haunts us day and night.

And that three-colour medal, purple, green and white,
slumped against the mantle clock, while you've been gone again.
*Thank God Joan of Arc wasn't married—*
that's what I sometimes say, as every time
I get you back, something more of you
has been stripped away, ounces, pounds, stones;
they've taken blood, hair, flesh,
exposed your nakedness.

*It's all for King and country,*
*how dare you make a fuss,*

*now the Kaiser's on the warpath,*
*once again it's 'them and us'!*

We can only stand by, patch up and mend,
expecting the worst,
as countless women have done for countless men.
Our roles reversed.

Honey, comfrey and calendula,
arnica, hot beef tea, how can we heal you, make you
strong enough now the Cat's released its Mouse,
you, home to us, to our house, to me?

As for you my battered darling, you're a woman out of time,
before your time, for all time,
right place, wrong time.
They say you choose what you do, but where is choice
when you are voiceless?
Where is choice when you are voiceless,
and when victory comes, where will you be?


*Simone Mansell Broome*

## Oh Cymru!

Oh Cymru made of skin and bone!
It's raining but we call it home
Built of iron, coal, slate and stone
From Bethesda down to Margam
They tried to put us on the dole
In 85 they closed the coal
But they didn't rob us of our soul
And we are still resisting.

Tower's worked its final shift
The Manics made our spirits lift
From Aneurin came a lasting gift
Ring the Bells of Rhymney !
Betty Campbell is in old Butetown
Shirley's in her sequined gown
John Cale has joined the Underground
He put the Zen in Cymru

Cordell wrote their wild history
In the Fire People of Merthyr,
Miners sang to set Paul Robeson free
Joe Herman drew their dignity.
Chelsea Manning told the truth to well
Now she' s alone in her prison cell
For this West Wales girl....ring out the bell
Set her free this morning!

Dic Penderyn and the Castle Inn
John Frost saw a world to win
Peace and Justice is no sin
From Cardiff they marched to Greenham
The immigrant and the refugee
Are welcome to our family

From fear and famine they did flee
And we are standing with them.

Oh Cymru made of skin and bone!
It's raining but we call it home
Built of iron, coal, steel and stone
From Bethesda down to Margam.

*Huw Pudner*

# Monuments

*(on the destruction of a Chartist mural, Newport, October 2013)*

People who demolish monuments—
turn tyrants into rubble
dodge bullets for their trouble
use hands instead of shovels
Make history
Struggle to be free
Overcome oppression
Deal with suppression
Inspire a generation
to go beyond their limitations
Reveal false democracy
As cruel fallacy

When politicians demolish monuments—
they employ workers at the double
behind a fence to ward off trouble
and confiscate the rubble
To suffocate dissent
in an attempt to represent
our monuments as just an eyesore
They never saw what I saw
A mural which upon inspection
charted our failed insurrection
A beacon of light in the dark
now butchered for a retail park

Chartists' demands never realised
The vote came piecemeal and bastardised
Piss ants who once claimed Chartist heritage
Sold out principles for patronage

Votes we fought for undermined
fair weather friends now resigned
to defending a system of privilege and profit
Backhanders are what they get off it
As Chartists fought against rotten boroughs
we must stand again with others
Fear no Gods, no masters, no borders
Oh, and 'perish the privileged orders!'


*Des Mannay*

## Arweinwyr gwrthryfel heddiw

Ac arthiodd un Arlywydd uchel ei gloch
wrth fenyw ym Mrasil ac un o'r Gyngres,
'Fyddwn i ddim  yn eich treisio chi
achos dy'ch chi ddim yn ei *haeddu!*'

Ac meddai Arlywydd arall  o'r Philipinau—
'gen i'r ateb da  sut i drin ffeminyddion
y rheiny  sy'n Gomiwnyddion trafferthus—
'Saethwch nhw  yn eu *camfflabats.*'*

A dwedodd cyn-Arlywydd  o'r Unol Daleithiau
 am wraig o'r  Wasg,' i waed lifo o rywle'
ac am ferch arall—gwadodd yn ffyrnig,
 'wnes i mo'i threisio , nid yw' fy *nheip i* '.

Sawl ochenaid sydd eisiau o enau ambell ddyn
 yn eiriau ar goedd neu floedd—a pha ffydd sydd—
pan gaiff merch ei threisio bob rhyw saith eiliad,
gan ddyn heb *deip* sy'n credu iddi ei *haeddu.*

A bydd penbwl o'r  Glas yn  sôn am 'fale drwg'—
Adda? A chyflwynydd ar deledu yn mynnu
nad yw 'merched marw yn newyddion erbyn heddi'.

Ac mae  Seneddwr  o bell  yn datgan yn fras
i fechgyn gael eu trin fel pe baen nhw  yn  bla,
a'r Chwith mor chwithig am greu byd 'tu hwnt i ddyn',
a'i gri dros lanciau unig sy am ddangos eu *gwrhydri.*

\*\*\*

Ac eto, mae merched  yn datgan  yn erbyn god o ddyn
wrth ganu'r byd o'r newydd dros *bob un*—ac fe ddaw yna ddydd
*Gododdin* newydd falle? Wedi tawelwch, elwch fydd'.

*Menna Elfyn*

*Camfflabats*: gair ar lafar am fagina.
*Aralleiriadl o'r Gododdin.*

## Found Poem: Gwrthryfel

And a President says to a female Senator,
face to face with so little grace,
'I wouldn't rape you because
 you don't *deserve* it'.

Another, the President of Manila
found a way to deal with *feministas*
who are also troublesome *communistas*—
'we'll shoot them in their vagina'.

And a former President tells the Press
of a journalist who asks tricky questions to impress
'there was blood coming out of' ...and another time
'I never raped the woman, she's just not my *type!*

How many quips does a man need to tell—
and what hope for women in the world when
every seven seconds some girl will meet her fate
and 'deserve' the descent of men from age to rage?

And some dick-head somewhere talks of 'bad apples,'
as the female journalist says *'dead women don't make the news anymore'*.
Elsewhere a well-bred Senator from Congress says with a straight face,
'boys are increasingly treated like an illness in search of a cure',

'The left are trying to bring about a world beyond men—
what in heaven's name—boys will be boys.' Amen.
And yet women are still here, refusing to lie down with lies,
singing the world alive—*'wedi tawelwch, elwch fydd.'*\*

*Menna Elfyn*

*Gododdin—a line which states: after great noise of battle there was silence. The line is reversed.*

(Translated by the author)

*wedi tawelwch, elwch fydd* / after silence, it shall be

## Ça Ira

It'll be fine, it'll be okay,
they sang as they swung on down the road
to make the world work a better way.

Freedom, equality, brotherhood,
everyone's dream, how could it fail,
once they'd cleared out the dead wood.

Only the axe was under a spell,
chopped and chopped and never let up,
like something out of a fairy tale,

and when they finally made it stop,
nobody had any appetite
for freedom; no one could handle hope.

It'll be fine, it'll be all right,
except that for now they've all slunk back
to where they were, or maybe not quite.

Perhaps just a small step down the track
can make a difference next time they try;
perhaps every ship that goes to wrack

is wood for a better. It could be
that men become wiser, that they shun
the evil they know, that history

is the tale of progress. Then again,
they might be like the vomiting cur
from the Bible. Yet... it'll be fine,

they sing, after every ruinous war,
each tyranny, pogrom, disastrous choice.
The axe chops on, till they remember

the magic words: poll, armistice,
uprising. Then they hand out freedom,
give folk doctoring, schooling, a voice,

welcome strangers into their home,
seeing their brothers. Though they turn
again to their folly, still it would seem

there's something in them that longs to learn,
that gropes for light, yet flinches away,
loving the glow, fearing the burn.

It'll be fine, it'll be okay,
freedom, equality, brotherhood,
it'll be fine, just not today.


*Sheenagh Pugh*

*From* **Paris: Summer 1968**

The 5th Republic
was still holding its breath
though the CS gas had cleared
and the famous cobblestones
were being hawked in Montparnasse
as souvenirs.
                Books
shoplifted from Shakespeare & Company,
paints from Gibert Jeune,
dropping bedrolls at dawn
from hotel windows
and scrounging meals
at the Sorbonne.

Under Pont St. Louis
strumming guitars
with Algerian boys
in flame-coloured flares,
in the 'Situationist's' garret
a 19 year old sociology student
'betrayed by the workers'.

In the Luxembourg Gardens
head on fire with LSD,
stunned by the geometry
of the tulip beds,
up every side street
the CRS
in hinged armour
like Futurist machinery.

*J.Brookes*

## M'aixeco, m'aixeco, m'aixeco...

No soc benvingut,
perquè parlo de la veritat punxant.
Parleu de solidaritat i igualtat
i mai compartiu el vostre pa.

Soc ignorat, soc demonitzat,
per confessar els vostres pecats.
Lluito en vers la injustícia,
lluito per no perdre el somriure.

M'aixeco, m'aixeco, m'aixeco,
de les flames de la por,
de l'escopinada de la hipocresia,
de les idees parlades....

T'omples la boca d'igualtat
i alimento els nens amb esperança.
Escrius sobre lluita i llibertat,
mentre pels pobres vesso sang.

Em demanes que voti vermell,
et demano que comparteixis el teu or.
M'apunyales a l'esquena,
t'obro el cor bondadosament.

I m'aixeco, m'aixeco, m'aixeco
fins que la respiració aturi la por,
fins que la pau sigui oxigen,
fins que la justícia no sigui una idea.

Fascineu la gent amb dolços,
els desperto del vostre postureig.
Robeu les esperances de la gent,
banyo les seves llagues cremants.

Seguiu venent fum,
jo bufo els vents de la justícia.
Em segueixes matant
i la gent mai m'ha oblidat!

I m'aixeco, m'aixeco, m'aixeco,
perquè la ràbia no s'esvaeix mai...


*Xavier Panadès I Blas*

# I rise, I rise, I rise...

I am not welcome anymore,
because I spoke a pungent truth.
You talk of solidarity and equality,
but you never share your bread.

I am ignored, I am demonised,
for exposing your sins.
I fight against injustice,
I fight to keep smiling.

I rise, I rise, I rise,
in the flames of fear,
in the spit of hypocrisy,
in spoken ideas...

You fill your mouth with equality,
while I feed kids with hope.
You write about freedom and struggle,
while I shed blood for the poor.

You want me to vote red,
I want you to share your gold.
You stab me in the back,
I freely open my heart.

Because I rise, I rise, I rise,
until breathing stops fear,
until peace becomes oxygen.
until justice is not just an idea.

You tantalise people with sweets,
I wake them up from your posturing.
You rob people's hopes
I bathe their burning sores.

You keep selling smoke,
I blow the winds of justice.
You keep killing me
but people have never forgotten me!

Yet I rise, I rise, I rise,
Because rage never fades...


*Xavier Panadès I Blas*

(Translated from Catalan by the author)

## Rising

Rising from the darkness
Rising from the earth
From the hearts that have been broken
By the tyrannies of birth

From the fields of indecision
From the battlefields of pain
From the shattered sheets of darkness
Burned so deep inside our brain

Rising from the furnaces
That blast our lives apart
From the shrapnel of the warfare
That indemnifies our hearts

Rising through the moonlight
Rising through the night
Rising through the visions
Of our wild and crazy sight

Rising from our prison cells
Rising from the jails
Rising for our freedoms
That are only out on bail

Rising against all circumstance
All twisted lies of law
Rising against hypocrisies
That feed the seeds of war

Rising against oppression
That sets us each on each
Rising against the walls of steel
That murders what we teach

For while there is injustice
And our people are not free
Your laws have no authority
Neither judgement nor decree

You need us: we do not need you
You vampires of our lives.
You thieves of all our energies:
You need us to survive

Like waves that crash upon the beach
We sanctify the prize
Our children bright come through the night
New generations rise

So stand aside, or else we'll force you
Out of the path we tread
To save the world is now our task
A price is on your head

The price is peace and justice
Our word is now our bond
So have the face to accept disgrace
Your time has gone


*Tim Evans*

## Women Rising

the castle looked beautiful even though it was in ruins
but even though the women might have looked beautiful
that was no good reason to photograph their dead bodies
for a cheap laugh

and though the waterfall cascaded down the steps
splashing white into the pool below
it should have been stained red to remember them by

and even though they want evidence to be clear,
it was not right to intimidate and interrogate women
especially black and poor women
and even though this night was heavy with rain,
and the listeners were drenched wet,
she spoke of lifelong fear and how it was
that the same fears were here now

and that even as she spoke, there was spiking going on
in the clubs nearby, and slapping and groping and stalking
and bruising and beating and strangling and unwanted sex
and shouting and swearing and terror
in flats and houses and businesses, all over

and though plain clothes would have guaranteed nothing
there were police in uniforms straining to hear what she had to say,
watching from the vans, unrepentant,
picking out the listening faces shivering under umbrellas

and in every town, there were vigils and rallies just like this
and in Dublin they won abortion rights
and in Glasgow, equal pay
and everywhere women are rising
for fairness

to be heard
believed
avenged

and afterwards, the candles went on flickering
in the shadow of the castle,
flames inside glass jars
and the women walked her back to her car
because she was afraid, and shouldn't have to be.


*Rhoda Thomas*

# Llwybr Rhyddid

*(ar gyfer alaw gan Rhydian Meilir)*

Dod o'r coed gan lusgo'n traed
Mewn cadwynau, a'n cefnau'n waed;
Ond ar ôl caethiwed hir—
Llwybr Rhyddid sy'n ein tir.

Roedd pob ffenest, pob drws ar glo;
Amhosib cyrraedd twll y to;
Ond fflach yr haul drwy grac y llen—
A Llwybr Rhyddid sy'n fy mhen.

Mae mynyddoedd yn y môr
A phob cwch achub sy'n man-o'-wôr,
Mae'r corff yn wan, mae coel er hyn,
Ar Lwybr Rhyddid yr ewyn gwyn.

Mi wn mai dyma'r dydd a'r awr,
Mae'r maes yn llawn a'r hwyliau'n fawr,
Mae sŵn ein chwerthin yn c'nesu'r gwaed,
Mae Llwybr Rhyddid dan ein traed.

*Myrddin ap Dafydd*

# The Path of Freedom

*(to a tune by Rhydian Meilir)*


From the woods we drag our feet
In chains, with our bloodied backs,
But after this long captivity
The path of freedom is our way.

Every window and door was locked,
Impossible to escape through a gap;
Yet slant of the sun through curtains
And the path of freedom beckons.

The waves are high as mountains,
Every lifeboat is a man o' war,
The body's weak but there's a hope
On the path of freedom's white foam.

I know this is surely day and hour
When the fertile field will flower
With laughter warming our blood:
The path of freedom's where we tread.


*Myrddin ap Dafydd*

(Translated by Mike Jenkins)

# Part 2

# Gwraidd / Origin

## Gwraidd / Origin

Flake surface slatescale overlap
dryripple silk, roughrub, exfoliation coarse
feels oddly comforting to finger whorls
agesweet dry tonguetip taste of sunbaked clag

Cracks crawl through blocks, snakefolds in frozen stone
broad undulating bands that glide
bluegreen waves glow through smoothdarkgrape
flowlines windblowing close to shore
some autumn spattered foolsgold rust

Primeval mantle lava flow
plutonic basalt pillars rise
longcooling granite firms below,
tectonic shifts as continents collide,
mountains shove free, seas rise and fall
new landmass, drifting North, welds Avalonia

fine grains: clay sand volcanic dust
settle as mud, congealing layers set as stone
hardsqueezed between colossal plates
mica quartz feldspar, crystallise,
rise from the guts of Wales to thrust in sky.

Chiselforce slicesplit, hammerhand hit
precise skill, plane cleave, straight and clean
holds sun for hours when skies grow dark.

*Anna Powell*

## Wales for Sale

I.

Houses are cheap here
ideal for second homes or Airbnb
cash cows, in prime locations

Many of our new neighbours
are from the same place as us
a home from home

Their estate agents favour us
we're willing to pay more
no need to wait to sell

Change the house name into
an English one, Welsh language mail
straight into the recycling

Ridiculous, moribund language
like something a hobbit would speak
sounds like they're clearing their throats

Maybe we'll start a little colony
our friends are interested
turn it into Cheshire-on-Sea

II.

I grew up in a seaside village
I can't afford to buy there now
house prices soaring

Local buyers outpriced
by those wanting second homes
buy to let, holiday rents

You'd think you were in England
in some neighbourhoods
the nicest ones, with the best views

I will look instead at the poor areas
down at heel, run down
far from sea and lakes

The Romans knew it, the strongest
always conquer, leave their mark
the defeated lose it all


*Annest Gwilym*


*Note: The title is a contradiction of Nid Yw Cymru ar Werth (Wales Is Not for Sale), a movement which seeks to address the current second homes crisis, which threatens the Welsh language and culture, as well as making house prices rise to levels unattainable for many native people.*

## Coal City

There are two ways of describing this city, at least two. I shall take one by the horns. There is a run of towers, all made from wood and assembled with dowels. They run south to northeast in chord that cuts the city's arc. They act as stands from which to observe the rough rugby that takes place on the city's many pitches. These games, if games they be, are always best observed from above. One of the bridges that carries access tracks bears a painted replica of the ancient days when there was only a single stadium and that of low capacity. The men depicted have sideburns and handlebar moustaches.

In the subdivisions of the streets spread out below like NASA photographs of Mars the men of the east often fight with those from the west. They dispute ownership and language. Their histories, they avow, are not the same. Drink sold from back rooms and street corners flows like the rivers.

In the north they keep their books in gapless stacks against the outer walls of their stone-built houses. Their fuel bills are light. I had a girlfriend from these latitudes once who told me that I was only interested in Jack Kerouac and talked of little else. It was a reasonable assumption at that time but now I have the ways this place works running in my blood.

The city has generating sheds in its southwest. These places smoke and scream. They endlessly light the skies with fire. They fill the air with grime, smudge, smuts, smog, smoulders, smoke, stain, steam, cinder, slag motes and ash. They have made the city, they know they have.

The centre of the city has many statues of the famous, often rendered astride their horses, bearing arms, holding binoculars. These reminders of ancient greatness, honour and obligation are, for most part, ignored by the lumpen. Their permanence has generated their invisibility.

To the south for a whole century there were black trucks, stacks, streams, streaks, dumps, and great bunds lining the docks used for loading. The workers spent their days filling themselves with the dust and their nights coughing it back. Nobody ever imagined it could end and now it has with no trace even in the tightest of cracks between the buildings no one can recall its name. There is an artwork near a place where there once was an oval dock that tries with its pit props and its lists of evocative resonating names but the substance itself makes no appearance. It is not spelled nor spoken. Fumbled. Lost.

On the way out where the light clothes of the visitors are still light and their hands as pink as when they were born questionnaires are completed. Surveys done. Why did you come? What drew you? What did you like most, are asked? The gaiety, they reply. And what made this place? To date no correct answer to that has ever been given.


*Peter Finch*

# The Drowned

Only cathedrals drown magnificently,
go down with a clamour of bell and steeple,

chime from sunken tombs, swallowed by
reservoir or ocean. Villages just return to the roots

that made them, voices silenced by a wrongness
of water, their windows flapping like trapped fish,

doors jammed and swollen. There is a rot here,
of book and wooden floor, chimney, casement,

a rubble of flooded lives; tree and bush washed
out of life, plants deflowered in their watery beds.

Sometimes they rise again, these lost kingdoms,
showing littered broken stones, forests

of ruined stumps in the shrinking back of tides.
Perhaps names had been carved into trunks,

scrawled on wallpaper; pictures drawn in chalk
by children who once played along these streets.

Now the drowned are bubbling up, floating through
our throats. Listen to the thousand angry tongues.


*Kathy Miles*

## Croesi Dyled Mehefin 1940

Annwyl Syr, yn ôl y sôn,
â'r haf yn dymor ofon,
cest fenthyciad: un wlad las,
un mynydd yn gymwynas
a Phabell heb ei phobol;
gofyn wyf, gaf i fe nôl?
Dwed, Frawd, o'th ranc cadfridog
a elli weld maint y llog,
y rhent tost sy' arnat ti
i linach plant Cilieni?
Wyth degawd, Frawd, bu'r lle'n frith
â siel gwn, —sisial gwenith
ddylai fod ar y ddôl fach,
nodau alaw dawelach.
Peintio 'nôl ein Hepynt ni
yn lân yw'n cais eleni,
a mynnwn nad hwn fydd haf
gwenoliaid y gân olaf.


*Mererid Hopwood*

# Crossing out the debt of June 1940

Dear Sir, I dare say you won't remember
that summer's fervour, when your fear
took out a loan, a green-blue land,
a borrowing, mountain sized,
a Pabell, without her people.
Well, here's the crack,
I'm writing since we want it back.
Say, Brother, from your general's rank,
d'you see the interest it's accrued,
the biting arrears that you owe
the lineage of Cilieni?
Eight decades, Brother,
the place has hissed with gun shell where wheat should sing sweet
silence.
So this letter, Brother,
claims our Epynt back.
We want to paint it free from hate's attack,
knowing, as we right the wrong,
we shall not let tomorrow
bring the swallow's final song.


*Mererid Hopwood*

(Translated by the author)

# Yellow

*(after 'When the Singing Stopped' by Karin Mear)*


a cage of feathers, light as breath, a flare
amid the groan and roar, a song
flung from the womb of the earth,
spark against the fading grey, a burst
of life from fragile lungs, seam
of yellow through each day, and
out, she comes, through paint,
through chalk, through wood, glass,
clay, through dance, through words,
bright against the black of coal—
this slim figure sings on, deep
beneath the surface of the world


*Rachel Carney*

# Tân

*(Diwrnod Glyndŵr, 16.9.20)*

Doedd heno, erbyn meddwl, ddim yn ddrwg;
cynuta wnes-i, 'hyd y lôn a'r ffos,
cyn gwylio'r priciau tamp yn magu mŵg
a chwalai fel telynau mud I'r nos.

O'r diwedd, chwythais nhw'n gymanfa dân—
rhyddhawyd heulwen hen, o fol y pren—
ac wrth gynhesu 'nghorff, a'r fflamau'n gân,
cymunais â'r gorffennol yn fy mhen.

O gwmpas tân fel hwn, mewn oes o'r blaen,
Datganai'r fflamau awdl-newid-byd;
synhwyrodd ein cyndadau'u ffordd ymlaen,
...a gwelaf mai yr un yw'r daith o hyd...
Mae fory 'Yes', s'n dal I'n haros ni,
yn chwythu tân Glyndŵr i 'nghalon i.

*Ifor ap Glyn*

# Fire

*(Glyndŵr's Day, 16.9.20)*

Tonight, it went much better than I'd hoped;
I'd gathered roadside kindling, since first light,
then watched it smoulder damply as it moped,
its smoke like silent harps adrift at night.

I blew it into roaring flame at last—
releasing ancient sun, from deep within—
and as I warmed myself, our long-lost past,
swelled up, like a cymanfa 'neath my skin.

Around a fire like this, in olden days,
our ancestors saw change in ev'ry flame;
a song to light their way, its lines ablaze,
...and I can see our journey's still the same;
Yes Cymru maps the road for our new start;
Glyndŵr still has the power to fire my heart.


*Ifor ap Glyn*

(Translated by the author)

*Cymanfa / Assembly*

## Adam

When dark foreboding clouds condense
to drop their blessings as a curse,
and righteous floods expunge our sins
for better or, more likely, worse,
will we regret the chances missed,
the loves unspent, the lips unkissed?
Will we repent our practised lies,
the silken fist, its thin disguise?
Or will we try to shift the blame
to innocents and victims all,
and never hang our heads in shame
but march aloof where we should crawl?
When will we start to do the work
that billionaires will not assume,
that politicians always shirk,
to plant and grow but not consume?
When will me make the burden ours?
Refuse to play the waiting game
the time we've left we count in hours,
so strive with unambiguous aim
to save what life the Earth has left,
to do what Adam was supposed
to do, not leave our home bereft
of nature and our sin exposed.


*Brian Phillips*

## Among Slavechildren, 1952

I sat among my schoolmates, bored to bits.
The teacher droned of Caesar and his wars.
Caesar and his conquests got on my tits.
Caesar was imperator of all bores.
The beak believed that we must be half-wits
to resist a long-dead empire's dusty laws
of grim grammar and even grimmer history.
They excited him no end, which was a mystery.

A boy came in and handed him a note.
He read, and frowned, dismissed the lad, then said
the king had died. A catch was in his throat.
He paused, and then repeated: "The king is dead."
He seemed to expect the class to pass a vote
of mortal sorrow. He willed our hearts to bleed.
Silence. Then one boy laughed. He found that shocking,
so socked him (he was very good at socking).

In Julius Caesar the best bit always was
when Brutus and the boys ganged up and stabbed
the bald old bugger, for he personifies
the Romans: anything not nailed down they nabbed.
Whole countries, their gods, their arts, philosophies—
anything grabbable the Romans grabbed.
King George was a Caesar, that was my belief,
so I had no cause to weep or wail, good grief.

The deceased, you understand, did no bad things.
It was one of our own, a chap named Henry Tudor,
who delivered us up to rule by foreign kings
and parliamentary potentates even shrewder
than Romans at serial theft and breaking-ins
(the Romans were good but their methods somewhat cruder).

Still, he was guilty of taking hefty wages
financed by burglaries of previous ages.

So there I was, with a Welshman telling me
stealing was fine if Caesar did the stealing
and living off crime's profits no felony
as long as kings were happy: most revealing.
That day I learned what quislings were, why we
were doomed to pass our days weighed down by the feeling
that being Welsh was hard, and bound to get
harder and harder still; impossible, yet.

For every tear that fell for George in Wales
left us a little more shrivelled in the soul,
and made more English our hills, our woods, our vales
as we descended deeper into the hole
where dark dulls identity till distinction fails.
O dinky miner's helmet, O craft-shop coal,
O lovespoon so elaborately tooled,
how can we know the rulers from the ruled?


*Alun Rees*

# Aneurin Bevan Memorial Stones

1.

Limestone was his rock
at Trefil, on Llangynidr Mountain,
on paths to the Chartists' Cave,
a dark mouth opening on a darker history,
articulate with the silence that filled it.

The stonechat heard him
and the ring ouzel among the rocks,
this young man with a stutter
declaiming Shakespeare or Marx,
correcting his voice, and honing it,
like a tool, useful as a miner's pick.

2.

His story is like an old myth
in a land of myth—
this monolith that was a man,
a boulder from the quarry where he walked,
and round him, three smaller stones,
his constituents, like petrified dancers,
the people he spoke to—
Ebbw Vale, Tredegar, Rhymney,
and, beyond them, the world.

3.

It is like a tale that begins
with poverty and ends with power:

Butcher's boy, miner, Minister
of State—one man
learning to speak for the people
he came from—miners,
steelworkers, families,
honing a tongue to bristle
and condemn, a voice with power to probe
the narrow privacies, and erode
the obdurate rock that is privilege.


4.


Limestone was his rock,
organic, soluble stuff, material
to shape a new world.

He would quote William Morris:
*Fellowship is life*
*and lack of fellowship is death.*

Man of flesh become stone,
this could not be a story that has an end.

The rock flakes away; the voice still speaks.


*Jeremy Hooker*

# The Underground Black

We were lucky with the weather.
Norah was born just up the hill
from Clydach bottom lake.
She pointed the street out
and we squinted into the sun.
The hooter went at 5 each morning
to rouse the miners.
Little girls soon learnt to sleep through.
A prehistoric pulley
dragged ton buckets of coal
past her bedroom window
all day every day.
Windows were frosted with soot.
Her ancient telly
showed shadows of the buckets
as they passed.
Soon, a railway was added
she said and it roared
with gravity down the hill,
aching with the weight.
In 1965 or 6, Norah said,
it collapsed.
Men were trapped for breath
and hugged and died
beneath our very feet.
Shaft A is still clearly marked.
If you lean over the marker
for shaft A and
listen close,
you can hear their voices rising
from the underground black
shouting for their wives,
their fathers,
their children.

*Jason Glover*

## Nomads

I am a follower in the footsteps of nomads,
they whispered to me 'keep moving Cariad' and I have.

I, like they, defined by the rhetoric of my day
Insisting, I must 'make work pay'
their empty words
tarnishes me
with the empty message they convey.

Driven from one solitary street to another,
from now on we'll only have each other.

I give my daughter a cwtsh swiftly
and with lessons learned, bitterly
I, too, by necessity, am a nomad
saying softly 'we keep moving Cariad,'
nothing changes—it never has.

*Gae Stenson*

*Cariad / Love*
*Cwtsh / hug*

# A Rhyme for the Gorbals Cooper

When Cressida tiptoed from Troilus' tent
And slipped into sleeping Diomedes' bed
"Don't ask me why, who on earth could have kent?
She just did! It is written." Chaucer said.
Just as enigmatic, a Chartist through
And through, walked from the Gorbals to Newport
To where Chartist numbers gathered and grew
Until as if it were some bloody sport
The thirty-seventh opened up. Honest men dead,
And honest men ran, the Cooper an' all
King's Men in pursuit, a price on his head,
And ran and ran from daybreak through nightfall.
And two years weary could run no more
Climbed aboard ship for America's shore.
Trekked to Dundee by Chicago, Illinois,
Observed the passing of counterfeit coin
And learned how it worked, the counterfeit ploy,
And so, being honest, turned them all in.
Put his honesty aboard the railroad
Foiled a plot to assassinate Lincoln,
Fired on strikers at Homestead, Union code
Anathema, cleaner, the code of the gun.
And hanged them Mollies. Now why would that be,
A Chartist against the people, Chartist
Friend to Carnegie and Gowen, buddy
To capitalism and capitalist.
A Chartist Eye that watches day and night
Now Pinkerton Eye, the Eye on the Right.


*Eric Morgan*

# Dennis

bullets rods arrows spears stones bombs
fall fury drench drown
strip silt cloud belly burst hills
breaks banks scours grass dumps crap

floods mercury meadows
plays Pooh Sticks with
wind whipped root ripped oaks
stone bridge chokes brickwork stripped

lifts slates steeple jacks chimney stacks
Met Office Red Warning two months rain in two days
flash gutters roll half-brick streams
hydraulic drains pop cast-iron fountains

floodplain estates play bumper cars
trespass old paths we tried to brick up
slops turds downstairs third time despair
floats uninsurable flotsam

sweeps man off feet
sirens all morning road blocked by boats
come looking come hooking out body
caught two counties down

twenty tips hidden heaps grown green
spoil turns liquid twice weight of water
spews down Tylorstown bleeds Aberfan black


*Phil Coleman*

## The One Percent

Thousands were making the precarious climb
up the front of the palace which appeared
three times the normal height,
to pay their respects
to the royals; they were numberless
salmon that had leapt the waterfalls
with their dying praise, it was innate.

There was television coverage:
with the sound off
the selection of shots
was a lesson in deference
to the celebs and toffs.
They were intimate and safe
to us. How remote
the relief of rage.

How we were schooled
in vacuous reverence:
it was something we did well,
it made us feel better
though tomorrow
we'd be worse off,
hung over, with for some
a bitter aftertaste,
a lurking sense
of being fleeced.

It was obvious who was to blame
once we'd tucked away the ambulances
and the bunting for the next time:
it was that something for nothing
generation.   How we yearned

for a smaller state
for the people just out of vision,
and welfare reform
for the malingerers we knew about
from the depth of our prompted being.

The wealth of the One Percent
grew bloated, out of proportion
as with water on the brain:
we share the cranial compression.
We missed the industrious
collusion offscreen.
We pay tribute to them,
the subliminal movers and shakers
with their quick fingers
at their soporific tricks.

We all pay too much tax.
It's decades now,
and the wisp of a stink of hocus-pocus
lingers behind us.


*Steve Griffiths*

## 'Coed-y-Twyn'

I'd galloped horseless all morning round
the field, dew shroud dampening my
knees. Heard the knock of croquet
balls, shouts from a neighbouring
farm then seen the cook with muscled
arms bite the dog in the unclean
kitchen.

"You rot in Hell as well," she snarled, pinning me
with her eyes then pushing her bloodstained
teeth beneath the tap. "Just like the rest of 'em."
And in midnight's darkness wandering from
my coffin bed that prophecy comes
true.

I'm in another land. Of Chinese whispers
from those porcelain dragons crouched
downstairs. Rain on the skylight, and cold
breaths of souls not yet released, snaking
under doors finding me, as if to say
"This is how it will be..."


*Sally Spedding*

## Waking up long ago

My father wasn't what you would call
in today's patois a woke man
but he had his moments all the same

my father would talk about Sir Walter Raleigh,
or Rowley, with some disdain
yet another plantation owner

who'd taken over Irish estates and lands,
it came as a surprise to find Ireland once called
by the name of "Isle of the Woods"

and the desecration paid out by the Elizabethans
of the destruction of all the green forests
of all the woods throughout Eire's green lands

The payment for resistance to colonialism
brutality, enslavement and plantations
people woke up to some things long ago
but how the story was told depended
on whether you were rich or poor
had the money or the power or not.

We can tell our own story,
it's ours to tell after all!


*Rob Cullen*

75

# Mother Zulu

And mother you told me of Zulus
during your South African stay
after the Malay evacuation
I think
you used the word *Zulu*
loosely
but it lit my seven-year mind

I saw Cullercoats full of them
at least versions who hunted
fish and talked another tongue
Their hands so unlike ours
that turned pages to read aloud
        you quoting Joyce Grenfell
           *We do so enjoy*
                *a well-delivered consonant*

The tread of language
marched out of books
        into my head


Try as I might
        to hold to your utterance
local speech was like Islay malt
           steeped in magic

The locals cast sonic spells
           which made me dizzy
        like the whisky years later would

Mouths gurgled
tongues rolled like waves
    and hell let loose
        once an argument started

Listening became a skill
    less for meaning
        more to sound

The same word said differently
greeted a friend or started a fight


I hung with the tribes and traded
*A tatie-heed half-nowt*
*skint an' scruffy*
*not a pot*
    *to pittle in*

Mother
how could anyone not fall
      loopy in love
    with such patter
that scampers and jingles
    without permission


*Ric Hool*

# Sitting Bull

*When I was a boy, the Sioux owned the world. The sun rose and set on their land;
they sent ten thousand men to battle. Where are the warriors today?*
—Tatanka-Iyotakae (Sitting Bull)

*More than 100 years after Custer discovered gold in our backyard, we're still finding
quality Black Hills Gold for you...*
—advertisement from Custer Gold, Inc.


After the Black Hills swung its gold watch
back and forth one absent-minded afternoon,
the hypnotized thousands arrived to pray
in the sacred folds and clefts, lifting up
their joyous spades, pans, and concealed weapons.

The buffalo objected
by removing themselves from history.
The prairie grass received a prophecy
of its trampling under black boots.
Water tried to be scarce.
The gold buried itself deeper in hidden veins
and in the grit of streams.
And the Black Hills remained,
as always, above the fray.

But Sitting Bull, torturing himself to a vision
in the Sun Dance, raised his slashed arms
and smiled as he watched dead cavalry soldiers
tumbling from the sky.

At Little Bighorn the hills wrapped around
Sitting Bull like God's own blanket.
He spied on the spies creeping through the grass
as if hunting extinct animals.

He listened to the good news that the wind carried.
He pitied the three lines of condemned horses
advancing their burdens of metal,
men, and ambition. Of their stilled bodies
Custer would make a steaming fort
for his last stand.

*David Lloyd*

## Un Dau Tri v. One Two Three?

Contrast. Always food banks and charity shops

Tories dressed by M&S, following "Brighton stick of rock!"

Drinks forever raised, as they never go away. No retirement for our struggle

Above the poverty line and the danger signs, this rise is to end that trouble

There is a feeling, it's in the air, information and debate

We are not the dying breed, we have interest? Not hate?

In our blood, our DNA, object to second hand and second rate

Certainly not the clowns that drown, via trickle down meant to seal our fate?


Ruffle the three feathers of a colonised slave

We sang our anthem felt proud, felt brave

Yet the patriotic idiot falls victim as the laugh was on us

We had no idea of meaning behind badge we all clutched?

Not a cheap whore for sale, just chained to pimps in H.Q

Release the beauty, kill the beast

It's up to us, that's me and you?

*John Williams*

# I Grow Deeper

At first water tickles as it trickles
Over river edge along stone fissures
Through muddy pools towards rock strewn gullies.
This titillation lasts but a minute
Soon swollen Teifi torrent overwhelms,
My green pathway quickly unpassable.
Millions of gallons of brown water
Swept on for miles from Strata Florida,
Llanbedr Pont Steffan, fields in between,
Washes dark soil from roots of mighty trees
Before tossing giants into maelstrom
Thence on to pile up at Henllan Bridge.
Many storms have ravaged my thoroughfare
Over hundreds of wet millennia.
Black agricultural plastic sheets drape
Leaf stripped branches alongside tattered white
Supermarket bags, orange nylon ropes,
Drowned sheep, smashed creosote-stained bothy walls,
All carried irresistibly forwards
In this rip-roaring Pandemonium
Into a new rock crushing existence.
Coracles and kayaks no more will ply
Gentle eddies and lazy green shallows.
The full force of Global warming horror
At last, finally, fully realised.
I am one defiled valley of many,
Where humans will never walk dogs again.
This is how life inevitably ends,
Sadly, mankind did bring it on themselves,
I grow deeper through sedimentary rocks.

*Harry Rogers*

# Eating at My Nan's

I remember Mahatma Gandhi
Breakfasting at my Nan's.
He was the perfect gentleman,
When we met we all shook hands.
He said that India would soon be free
From the British Empire's choke;
And India would be a superpower
When it threw off that yoke.

I remember Nelson Mandela
He and my Nan had lunch.
They talked about apartheid;
It would end soon, was his hunch.
Black and white would be equal,
Everyone would get a vote,
South Africa would look forward.
It was his greatest hope

I remember Arthur Scargill,
He came to my Nan's for tea,
Before the miners' strike started—
I think it was eighty-three.
They talked about the government
And the attacks on the working class
And disappearing freedom—
I think it will come to pass.

I remember Muhammad Ali.
He had dinner at my Nan's,
She'd cooked a special goat stew
They talked about Vietnam.
He said he'd fight no wars abroad,
They're not the enemy;

The real opponents are at home.
It made real sense to me.

I remember Che Guevara
At my Nan's for his late night meal.
He spoke about Cuba's freedom—
I couldn't believe it was real.
They'd kick out the corrupt, he said,
And the people would be free.
I said it was a great ideal,
But we'd have to wait and see.

 I remember eating at my Nan's,
With politics the fayre.
With tales of fighting for freedom,
For bread and for clean air,
For education and our health
And a right to vote for change,
For freedom from starvation.
Does that seem very strange?


*Peter Jones*

# Aber-fan a Phontyberem

*(claddwyd Dyfrig Hayes, 9 mlwydd oed, ym Mhontyberem)*

Mewn cornel o'r Bont lle mae'r coed yn grwm
yng nghil llygaid ceir sy'n llifo drwy'r stryd,
fe gladdwyd un mab yn naear y cwm.

Aber-fan a'r Bont mewn galar ynghlwm,
dau le yn cwrdd fel dwy law'n dod ynghyd,
mewn cornel o'r Bont lle mae'r coed yn grwm.

Un wyneb mewn gwers a'r rhuthr fel drwm
a'i guriadau'n gadael rhieni'n fud,
fe gladdwyd un mab yn naear y cwm.

Mae'r dail yn disgyn fel punnoedd pob swm,
rhieini'n gwylio dros fedd fel dros grud
mewn cornel o'r Bont lle mae'r coed yn grwm.

Dau le fel dau riant a'u galar trwm
yn wynt sy'n chwibanu a chodi cryd
ers claddu un mab yn naear y cwm.

Rhesi beddau gwynion ar y llethr llwm
yn sibrwd hwiangerdd am warth i'r byd;
mewn cornel o'r Bont lle mae'r coed yn grwm
fe gladdwyd un mab yn naear y cwm.

*Aneirin Karadog*

# Aberfan and Pontyberem

*(Dyfrig Hayes, aged 9, was buried in Pontyberem)*

In a corner of Bont where the trees wail,
Through the corner of eyes of passing cars,
One son was buried in the earth of this vale

Aberfan and Bont intertwined in their grief,
Two places meet like two hands meet to pray
In a corner of Bont where the trees wail.

One face in a class and the rush a drum roll,
Its beats leaving parents unable to speak;
One son was buried in the earth of this vale.

The leaves fall like money meaning nothing at all,
Parents watching over a grave as if over the cot
In a corner of Bont where the trees wail.

Two places like two parents arm in arm in grief,
A wind that whistles and makes your skin crawl
Since one son was buried in the earth of this vale.

White graves in line on the slope of the hill
whispering a lullaby of this world's disgrace
In a corner of Bont where the trees wail,
One son was buried in the earth of this vale.

*Aneirin Karadog*

(Translated by the author)

# Part 3

# Protest

# The Protest: Welsh Miner, 1926

I can see you now,
Sitting in your home
In the poor valleys,
Your anger burning
In the pit of your belly,
For the workers exploited
By the moneyed mine owners.

I can see you lacing your boots,
As you get ready
To go to the march through the town,
Sprawled beneath a shadowing mountain,
Where the morning sun eases
The drab rows of houses,
Where the church that is locked, the school silent.

You walk out into the day
And greet fellow miners
As they leave neighbouring homes.
Drums and kazoos can already be heard.
A dark bird darts to the safety of the trees.
You head to the congregation
Of banners and placards,

To the steadfast music of protest.
Women and children are lined along
The pavements, their smiles and clapping
Challenging the poverty of their existence,
A dog barks loudly in a garden.
As your fearless carnival of hope
Moves up towards the colliery.

*Peter Thabit Jones*

## Class War Saint

Makhno's photo hangs
alongside
my uncle's: same cheekbones,
scythe eyes.

*We were peasants then,*
the last time we were together.

*May the hands and hearts*
*crushed for wages*
*be avenged.*


*M.S. Evans*

# Gorymdeithio

Roeddent am ein torri,
ein pellhau oddi wrth ein
hunain a'n gilydd, rhwygiadau
yn dyfnhau rhyngom.
Ein trwytho ag ofn, dicter, casineb
*rhywun arall sydd ar fai, bob tro.*
Roedden nhw eisiau distawrwydd, neb
i gwestiynu pam bod gwahaniaeth
yn broblem, yn bryder, bygythiad.
Nid yw distawrwydd yn siapio ein dyfodol
nac yn difa'r casineb a yrrir gan anfodlonrwydd.
Gwyliwch ni yn ymgynnull, gwrandewch
ar sŵn ein traed, fel eraill a fu o'n
blaenau yn gorymdeithio,
oherwydd gwyddom bod hyn yn iawn.
Mae ein lleisiau'n dod at ei gilydd,
yn chwyddo'n uwch na'r
blwch pleidleisio. Ymunwch â ni,
gorymdeithiwch yn y man lle sefwch.
Ni allant anwybyddu pob un ohonom.

*Ness Owen*

# March

They wanted us broken,
stranded away from our-
selves and each other, rifts
deepening between us.
Drip-fed fear, anger, hate
*it's always someone else's fault.*
They wanted silence, no-one
to question why difference is
a problem, a worry, a threat.
Silence won't shape our future
end hate-driven discontent.
Watch us gathering, hear
the tread of our feet, like
others before us marching
for what we know is right.
Our voices not alone but
amplified louder than
the ballot box. Join us,
march where you're standing.
They can't ignore us all.


*Ness Owen*

(Translated by the author)

# Turning points

See the poor man's cow burn
hear scorching sheep scream.
Watch news films of the world on fire
from behind our various screens.

Trees crackling, bark burning, lumber falling
heat coursing across hills
that could be our Preselis or our Brecons,
our Cambrian mountains blackened.

*We will him on, that man with the cow.*
*Turn around, turn to home*

Grab your kids, your mama and grandma
leave your photos, all the pictures on the walls
see them burn, see them burn
run to the sea, run run run.

Smoke chokes your lungs, sears your throat
inferno follows you
an avalanche of fire down the mountain
closer and closer rolling and rolling

*Turn and turn again, watch your life burn.*

Your neighbour's cow is on a rein, her bulging eyes askance
his father has the dog, dead lizards scatter the path.
A small child carries a tortoise.
See people on the shore—
friends, cousins, brothers and sisters and all their children
soot smudged across faces, eyes vacant
yet full of fear.

*Turn, look back.*

A wall of orange rages closer and closer
rolling smoke wreaths around
blackens your trees,  kills your bees
swallows your village.

Ash falls like snowflakes, shifting footprints on sand
where sea is grey mud.
*Turn* to the boats, the only way
to escape from heat and smoke.

*Now turn again, turn again.*

Look to your governments,
those who would let all our futures burn.
Let them see your dark staring eyes
your lost and angry faces
your fear and despair.
Hold their gaze.
Make them turn to you.
Do not let them turn away.


*Jackie Biggs*

## Right to protest

The right to our freedoms
Lays on our heads
This law the draconian thugs want to bring in
Taking away our rights to speak pre-pandemic
We were standing at Castle Square united as one.
Now we are fearful we will be watched and stopped
For the rights of our freedoms
Which lays on our heads
This government don't care
Violence is their game
If it's all the same
From slavery to women's rights
They don't want us to fight.
But we must not give in to them
We must raise our hands
Speak loudly
Write poetry and more
For it's our right to protest.


*Samantha Mansi*

# Kill the Bill

*For Seren-Haf, my daughter's friend*

The streetlamp spotlights
her white coat in the crowd.
Blonde hair.
Back to the dizzy blur
of the phone camera.
Iconic,
chessboard princess,
facing a dark line of menacing silhouettes.

"Why are you asking us to move?"
she inquires, politely, innocently.

The response does not answer her question
but is blatant crushing proof of the rationale for protesting.
Smash!
The riot shield fells her.
Ugly head shock,
drop, jostle, stop.
Broken phone.
Screaming chaos & shadows.
Perspective gone.
Moral compass lost.

But after the camera lies blind & silent
video evidence is salvaged.
Incendiary.
And she is lifted by her friends,
bruised resilient & splendid,
elevated by belief & defended by love.
Transcendent,
a rising star.

*Rosy Wood-Bevan*

## Hope Shifts

Say goodbye
We've been living in the old world far too long
Reboot, give a hoot, shoot the old world in the foot
Each living cell, each drop of water,
Each periodic element isn't
Mine them, sell them; old school mind-sets
White patriarchy's icy shadows
Now's the time—shift out of the way
Let abundant light reach us all
Warm our various skins, green bones and jaded souls
Let us hear let us see let us feel
Let us breathe let us be
Put away our fears and hear the truth of others
Really, really listen... and...
Someday soon we may awaken *to a world with a future...*


*Caroline Richards*

## Austerity Bites

There is something in the air
and we breathe it every day
a war of attrition
an ugly game of lies
as the politics of austerity
bites and pinches our lives.

Today, this country
is no gentle place
the sky full of Tory toxicity
as they tear apart the welfare state
and so much more.

Easy to lose control
trying to feed hungry hearts
all we need is love they say
but on poverty's line
it's the only thing
we have now for free.

It feels like 1979 again
but with more of a sting
as politicians' pickpocket
daily from our purse
and banker's bonuses still pile high.

Silence is not golden
time for them to hear us shout
beyond their false mirrors
no use just complaining
in the darkness we must sow light
as they treat us with derision
time to drive these bastards out.


*Dave Rendle*

# Come the Revolution

If no-one else can make it, call on me
To light the flares or man the barricades;
Most afternoons I'm likely to be free
To keep the peace on partisan parades,
Bold tarmacadam camaraderie
Of placards, chants and vegetable grenades.

Give me a cause, show me some condemned field,
Point me towards the sound of truncheons and
My Co-op shoes will do the talking. Yield
No inch to tinpot despots. Take my hand,
Companions with those scars that never healed,
From Aldermaston to the Holy Land.

Badges in multiplicity bedecked,
Pure and progressive pearly kings and queens,
Proud souvenirs of routes that may connect
Anti-apartheid, children's rights, lush scenes
Environmental, dogs of war unchecked,
Taxed polls, gay pride, quixotic might-have-beens.

Yes, I have kept the faith, I still believe
In people power: freedom to roam about
The moor, within the common law, and leave
Nought but our tracks behind. Gladly lose out
On each transaction and, from that, conceive
Rich rights-of-way around misrule's redoubt.

*Mike Douse*

# The American pastime (on the 4th of July)

I saw the best minds of your generation destroyed by
a red, white and blue narrative
excluding the black, brown and native
Americans who decant
their history like wine
drunk from glass houses
you threw stones from,
built by the founding fathers
across to the Wild Wild West
emblazoned with a crest of rifles
and in the crosshairs
you hunted caribou, buffalo and wolves
howling at the new moon,
in the New World that did not belong to you.
But you claimed it regardless
as the red men brought gifts
so you'd survive
and passed around a peace pipe,
you raised a flag
as you slept under the
Stars and Stripes
keeping your face always toward the sunshine
as shadows fall behind you,
across that great frontier
mustangs bucking,
banners blowing in the wind
as you buried its heart at Wounded Knee.

Four score and seven years later,
a Constitution,
establishing, emancipating and assassinating,
blacklisting and whitewashing from a White House
while watching strange fruit hang

from the poplar trees
at the hands of the great white calling,
but you had a dream
made a stand by refusing
from your bus seat,
crossing bridges of racial tensions,
civil righting wrongs
and singing songs by troubadours
under the shimmering skylines,
skyscrapers, tenements and ghettos
the suburbs, the plains, the mountains,
the monuments, memorials and statues
along Route 66 through your national parks.

America's pastime is not baseball,
your Hollywood hall of fame
is a different game
on the big screen you see but you don't talk
about colouring schoolkids outlines in chalk
counting backpacks stacked like barricades
blocking gun reform
because it's cemented
in the foundations of a nation
that seems to care less and less,
You speak in podium statements that make no sense,
in a tweet or on the page.
Instead of the dawn of a new age,
You're still trigger happy
to see an apparently illegal baby in a cage
a TV star in the top spot
and a shock jock taking potshots
at protesters fighting for a future
brighter than Edison's lightbulb
not stolen like Tesla's Inventions,
where the next generation celebrate
not being shot before they graduate.

And yet
pledging allegiance to a flag
that gave you your Bill of Rights,
to religion, to free speech and to bear arms
from the cities to the farms,
the disparity of rights is immense.
There's no sitting on fences.
You erect them with barbed wire coils
and rally to build walls
and while tensions boil
your elected officials call for
teachers to be armed
to protect the innocent from pain
and blow away the bad guy
like Dirty Harry or John Wayne.
To swap trigonometry for trigger knowledge
See the warning signs of a past pupil's
Facebook post or past reports
from when they were ten
that say "May take an AK47 into a Kindergarten"
but though tears over bloodshed
is sadly nothing new.
Be prepared to find post-truth YouTube
false flag conspiracies
that what they saw, they didn't see
to look dead kids' parents in the eyes
and tell them that it didn't happen,
that a film crew created a blood splattered class
crushed crayons into the carpet of shattered glass,
shouted action and got actors to lay
where these make-believe children should be safe to play,
'cause the NRA say the CIA used CGI to fool the USA
that all mass shooting victims up in heaven
who kept their hands in the air
deserve your thoughts and prayers

(and you should send 'em)
but don't you dare change that second amendment
cause you still want to buy a Uzi in a 7/11
ammo at Walmart and caskets at Costco
and while the bullet proof ignorance of Congress
was paid for by your hypocrisy.
Oh, say can you see
by the dawn's early light
what is your god damn right
to do or say
on this,
your Independence Day?


*Siôn Tomos Owen*

# Colston, Bristol, 2020

They tore down the statue of the slave trader,
From the plinth where he had lorded it
For centuries over their city,
Trampled underfoot by protestors,
Just like he had trampled their ancestors.

84,000 men, women and children
Torn from their homes, human cargo
Crammed into the hold, for eight
Weeks at a time – 19,000
Never survived the journey.

The white man who had profited
From their sweated labour,
Silver spoons for the sugar
He ladled from broken backs:
*'One of the most virtuous
And wise sons of the city'*
Dipping his fingers in the
Blood of injustice.

With ropes and pulleys,
The protestors brought him down,
Graffitied his body with political slogans,
And pitched him into the very same dock
From which he sailed his ship of human cargo.
Poetic justice? I think so.

And if it bothers you, this empty plinth,
If you think seeing something forcibly
Removed from the place where it belongs
Is wrong... just imagine how you'd feel,
If the same thing happened to a human being,

For someone else's financial gain?

Good riddance, Edward Colston,
We'll not miss you,
May we never see
The likes of you
Again.


*Rebecca Lowe*

# Part 4

# Crynu / Shiver

# Shiver

Home of secrets, splattered
with shock-vomit. Always the litter
of a lie. Flowers fade here—
ground rifted to falter.

But the good-bride plan—
the mother of all
is firing up tea. Always
smiling into the parch,
in sickness and in health.

Lips blistered, muscles revved,
she steers her animus—antler tipped,
from his entrapment.
Dawn is so liberating.

It's the wool of other women
that keeps her on the back of it,
how they end her stories,
wrap children with a shiver
into their chests.

Tracking wood's map,
she washes from springs, eats petals
glossed with summer. Earth to hem
again. She holds yin, a rising

voice from her pelvis. Rain—
diamonds on every hair and finger.


*Guinevere Clark*

## Every 30 Seconds

His expression was a bad sign
An omen of a hard time
Casting shadows of doom
On the bright, sunlit room

Mentally preparing her exit
Potential mind mines predicted
Before explosions of wrath
Besiege her treacherous path

Insults roar, this sudden storm
Like a flash, true to form
Fear-freezed, feeling floored
Eyes fleetingly flick to the door

Soon objects in full flight
Missiles thrown with all might
Bombarded with hatred, ill strife
Her body a constant jackknife

If lucky enough, her escape
Will be reached before fists rage
On her core, avoid bruising
nobody sees. Before losing

her sanity, losing her soul
Reach safety before being swallowed up whole
If she's lucky he'll drop dead
Witness his exploding head

its tenebrous contents rancid, pitch black
A canvas viewed publicly, exposed his attack
A mirror held up to his weak cowardice
Surely comeuppance, should karma exist

Inevitably his blue calm manifests
as she leaves, his Sunday-best
manners, full of drama to witness
All lachrymose, begging forgiveness

Promises made with no grain of intent
She should know his behaviour's not really meant
One day she'll find strength to leave him for good
He'll rot in self-pity, so-called misunderstood

*Mary Kaye*

*Note: Every 30 seconds, a woman rings a domestic abuse helpline*

## I'll Never Stay at The Dorchester

I'll never stay at the Dorchester
it's built on stones of death
Sharia law is an evil force
in the hands of evil men
if you kill in the name of god
it's murder just the same
Milly and Mo, Jack and Joe
there's no crime in being gay
Deuteronomy is ancient history
we don't sacrifice goats today
Milly and Mo, Jack and Joe
there's no crime in being gay

Woman or man, womanly man
manly woman or trans
stitch something on, turn it inside out,
cut them off or have implants
it's right to be whoever you are
live your life, take your own stance
for personality in all reality
is in your head not in your pants
Deuteronomy is ancient history
we don't sacrifice goats today
Milly and Mo, Jack and Joe
there's no crime in being gay

Sisters and brothers and all the others
LGBTQ+
every pebble that's thrown at one
is a rock cast at all of us
invincibility in solidarity
our mettle you can't even rust
geeks and freaks, one-off uniques

unlost, in odd we trust
Deuteronomy is ancient history
we don't sacrifice goats today
Milly and Mo, Jack and Joe
there's no crime in being gay

I'll never stay at the Dorchester

*Karen Gemma Brewer*

# The Mud Service

So, this is us, a little corner of the fat land,
still talking in our zombie tongue,
still clinging to the accents that they can't decode
unless we pare them down, dampen the consonants,
sharpen the vowels. We are landfill,
and Britannia puts whisky in our evening feed,
lies us down in our bed, face down on the mattress
though she knows she shouldn't chance it,
our drowsiness unnatural, our breathing silent.

Puts camouflage on her dry cheeks,
dresses in secrets (the one with the zip-through middle
she keeps for business). She says,
Always be prepared to turn tricks for the sailors.
They will put their dirty hands on you, in you,
they will stuff you full of Sovereigns.
Let them empty themselves in your depths.
Open up, good girl.
Old girl, who never grows old.

The year the mud was scraped and sunk,
phosphorescence illuminated the coast.
It said, Look for the boat with the split lip
dropping its load in the darkness,
lighting the way from Hinkley Point to Penarth Head,
then home to a power-station breakfast.
And we swam in its wisdom.
Soundlessly. Wordlessly.
The beds beneath us shifting.
Bad mother.
Bad mother.
Bad mother.

*Tracey Rhys*

# Goddess Pose

In this pose                        we are all woman
primal             standing
unapologetic
legs apart
squatting
arms open
hands splayed
cactus style
yes, we wear leggings
yes, you can see every sinew
yes, we have crotches
guess what, mister
I can see yours        inside your joggers
when you do        your squats
and yes, we have      these breasts
made for suckling     our children
supported in        crop tops
not for you         to photograph
and no, we will       not hide them
'cos in this pose        we rise.

*Adele Cordner*

## Behind locked doors

She sat on the pavement,
her clothes in two Co-op carrier bags.
He had kicked her out again.
She rattled the door of the flat.
A light winked through an upstairs window.
But he did not come down to let her in.
"It happens all the time,"
said a neighbour across the road.
"One night she was out there starkers.
A man passing by gave her his jacket."
The woman, hair tied back,
and clad in the usual tracksuit
stayed there defiant as the wind blew
and uncovered her few possessions.
Then a bus came around the corner
and she ran to catch it,
the Co-op bags advertising their special offers.
I wondered would she go back there.
She always did, I was told,
caught up in a loop of abuse.
But where else could she go?
Two people thrown together,
clinging on to a little hope
in their world of darkness.
How many more are there like her,
Hidden by curtains, unheard in street noise?
The same old story played day by day,
the hopeless life in a hopeless world
while neighbours shake their heads
and close their front doors.


*Phil Howells*

# Epidemic

Their names are penned like a grocery list
Pinned to a cold fridge door:
☐ Sarah
☐ Sabina
☐ Julia
☐ Jade
And God knows how many more.

Attractive women, in their prime,
All taken far too soon.
Innocent victims of heinous crime
Gone, through no fault of their own.

Precious lives, just walking home
Fall foul to danger lurking;
Fear enforced, nowhere to turn
Entrapped by lone wolves in sheep's clothing.

*This one's* hiding in full plain sight
Deceit disguised with a smile.
Horror served, in broad daylight.
Don't believe him, *RUN A MILE.*

*That one*, recognise the third-rate script
Quoting lines from a Z-list movie:
'Hello Darling, fancy a lift?'
'Oi Babe, like a lick-le sweetie?'

*So how-do-I-tell?*
Is 'Psycho' that man in the scruffy white van
Dressed as your Uncle Dell?
Or dishy date disguised as 'best mate'?
Are you Norman Bates from hell?

All the while, in sleepy Pyle
Dippy Dappy, boy-next-door
Brewing bile with a sneering smile
Grabs a remote off a living room floor.

Glued to Netflix, needs a fix
'Teach me, evil masters of crime!'
Unzipped trousers, flicks and picks
Killer Thriller series 9.

Lesson over, revision slate
(A checklist ticked on a packet of fags)
Stuck with Sello by the fiery grate:
☐ Fill car boot – tools, black bags √
☐ Duct tape – great √
☐ Sugar lumps – bait √
☐ Rope – checkmate √


*Kitty Jay*

# The Coloured Girl Speaks of the Colour of Words

*'Emancipate yourself from mental slavery*
*None but ourselves can free our mind'*

—Bob Marley, 'Redemption Song'


I
could say that I was not black enough
or white enough
or woman enough
or man enough
or mother enough
or father enough
or innocent enough
or enlightened enough
or political enough
or culturally active enough
or pinned to the body-mast enough
or whalebone to the sea enough
in the microplastic tsunami of my generation
I
could say that I was not lyrical enough
or raw spitting spoken-word enough
to sprinkle my poems with anger
or the right to be born of woman
I could wash my hands right now
—Lady Macbeth of the West Indies—
of the small murders and intimacies on the way to becoming
someone's native
someone's definition of any drop of existentialist blood
that made me what I am

I could blame any lover for the lack of me
anyone who sees my colour before they see me

anyone in the tick-box of power
who placed me in the tick-box of Other
those in the plantation chair rocking on white verandas
would have me remain in the shadows of the greenheart tree
that I would never be white enough
or black enough
or acid-tongued enough
or representative enough
to package or market
to transfer the guilt of generations
that lurk beneath each ejaculation.

But the suitcase I carried from the New World to the Old
was made of alligator skin
seamed with the unwritten tears and strangled voices
of those whose colour was all washed out
stained to an indeterminate brown of rivers and semen
so muddy, their language became the scream of capuchins
the burning ash of cane
the muzzle of the manatee
the roots of the banana tree where
Aloysius Benedictine lies buried
the noose still around his neck.

But
our language is also
the vibration of home-made guitars
the self-taught melody of mouth organs
the ornate passage of tabernacles
the inkstained hallelujahs whose
proclamations of promise
rise high in the Amens of the faithful
high in the signatures of egrets across
a Demerara evening sky
high in the creativity of those who dare to inscribe

their dreams like oil on water in the mouth of the Orinoco
high with the words of Marley
Emancipate yourself from mental slavery
None but ourselves can free our minds ...
So          this is a Praise Song for the enough of us
we are enough in the transcribing of us
we are enough
we are enough
I        am enough.


*Maggie Harris*

# I AM WARMAN

I am not your girl not your baby your sugar nor pearl. I am not a shoulder nor an ear to listen. I am not a point to be scored nor a notch to be bed-posted. I am not a weapon to be fired nor a gadget to be poked then tossed in a cabinet. I am not a target to be tracked then attacked in the dead of the night. I am not your luv nor am I hun or even 'a bit of fun.' I am not a filtered selfie bootie to be swiped, nor a pointless emoji to be typed. I am not a girl for you to call nor a supplement to your narcissistic caustic ego-self. I am not a pussy to be pounded. Do I look like a tissue to wipe away your explosion of sorry ejaculation? I see the bombshells of nihilism which occupy, nullify the shallows of your unexplored being. I fought my way out of the womb, past the perils of my girlhood bed, through the history we have read. Low-bred, I have gone unfed. Bled for these words to be said. I am not your girl. I am Warman: a woman who has fight!

*Gemma June Howell*

123

# Part 5

## Agorwch eich llygaid / Open your eyes

## Just a Smack at the Manics

The air breaks open
onto an emptiness

the memory of an empire
not too big, just small

enough to patronise
tired of being tired

and fucked by being
fucked, shafted rather

by the impotent cant
of bigots, a tiny country

hardly worthy of the name
where a trans woman's

an identity crisis
in a frock, a gay man

still bent as an S-hook
whispered after, after

dark. Say yes
to ourselves and

you'll need a UKIP
mask and a Dai-cap

a wife at the sink
and an antivax

certificate from
the university

of piss bugger all

the air breaks open
you can visualise it

clouds opening
valleys down below

houses close together
just like our hearts

open your eyes
really open them

and hopefully
you'll find

there's more
to us than that,

a heart
still weeping tears

and attuned to the harp of love


*Julian Meek*

# The Mask of Sanity: June 2020

As I stayed home in lockdown Wales
While drought and sun gave way to gales,
The unprecedented times
Begged an echo in my rhymes.

I met Privilege *en route*
To his weekly photoshoot—
Disguised as a Prime Minister—
And then things got more sinister.

His adviser, Laughing Boy,
Who treated strict rules like a toy,
Kept his job though everyone
Said he should go for what he'd done.

News came from across the sea
Of such police brutality
When George Floyd was killed with hate,
Crowds came out to demonstrate,

Which only made the resident
Idiot in the White House, President
Chump, tweet that when looting
Starts, so rightly does the shooting.

In Britain, France, and Germany
They marched in solidarity,
Not silence but a shout and clatter
Making known that Black Lives Matter.

You mustn't gather, said the Clown
Who had told us that lockdown
Still applied to everyone
But Laughing Boy—now let's move on!

Home Secretary Priti Patel
Thought she had the right to tell
Other BAMES to hold their tongue—
She'd been abused when she was young,

She said, and still had a career
In P R, lobbying for beer
And the tobacco industry—
Why can't you all succeed like me?

But folk ignored the government,
Fed up with seeing the rules bent,
And living with a public statue
Black people felt was sneering at you.

They hauled the image of the slaver
Down and threw it in the river.
They started to consider Nelson,
An imperialist with bells on,

And Churchill, who was yet another.
Every slave is like my brother
Or sister, so they said, arise
They said, there is no prize

For putting up a moment longer
With the powers that may be stronger
At the moment but will not
Remain so now they've lost the plot.

Out came the English Nationalists
Some of them leading with their fists,
Getting into fights till one
Got hurt, and had nowhere to run,

But Patrick Hutchinson carried him
Over his shoulder, looking grim,
To safety where riot police
Made sure he stayed still in one piece.

The photograph of this event—
*Black man rescues right-wing gent*—
Went viral, and began to offer
Hope at last, to those who suffer,

That reconciliation might
Be the outcome, not more fights.
But still the government was awful
And made starving children lawful,

Ignoring a broad-based campaign
Requesting that they think again,
Until a footballer joined in
And told them quite how poor he'd been.

His mum had done all that she could,
But without that free school food
Marcus Rashford never would
Have been a star, or even good.

The government did another U-turn
Which caused Laughing Boy to gurn—
But as that was his usual face
The fact escaped the human race.

Then Greta Thunberg said, we've seen,
Reacting to Covid 19,
The world act when it knows it must,
And people rising from the dust

In mass action for BLM
Can confront an ancient problem.
Now let's rise up for action,
Not for any sect or faction

But world-wide justice, and the planet.
A spark is lit, it's time to fan it!
There's no time to waste or lose.
Let us fill our boots like heroes!

Then she quoted lines she'd learned
By heart in the days she yearned
For a world that would awake,
See what action it should take,
And at last a difference make:

*"And these words shall then become*
*Like oppression's thundered doom*
*Ringing through each heart and brain*
*Heard again—again—again—*

*"Rise like lions after slumber*
*In unvanquishable number—*
*Shake your chains to earth like dew*
*Which in sleep had fallen on you—*
*Ye are many, they are few."*

*John Freeman*

## Gelliwastad ar Dân

Odd hi'n nosi, ac er nad odd
hi'n haf eto doedd hi heb lawio
ers tipyn ac odd y gwynt
wedi bod yn chwythu
o'r gogledd-ddwyrain fi'n credu
a gadael yr eithin yn sych.

Ond o'n i methu gweld yr eithin chwaith
achos odd yr haul yn rhy isel
ac odd hi'n fwy o wyll na nos na dydd
a hefyd odd popeth ar dân.

Ond nes di godi dy ddwylo tua'r sêr
a gweiddi a 'nes I'r un peth a gweiddi
ar y mynydd i beidio ond dodd e ddim yn gwrando
arnon ni, er bod ni'n hen ffrindie
dodd e ddim yn gwrando

A beth arall allen ni 'di neud ond gweiddi?
Dodd dim byd arall
a nath e losgi'n ddu.


*Dyfan Lewis*

## Gelliwastad Ablaze

Night was falling, and though
it wasn't summer yet it hadn't rained
for a while and the wind
had been blowing from the northeast
I think, leaving the gorse dry.

But I couldn't see the gorse either
'cause the sun was too low
and it was more dusk than night or day
and everything was ablaze.

But you raised your hands towards the sky
and howled and I did the same and howled
at the mountain to stop, but it wouldn't listen
to us, though we were old friends
it wouldn't listen.

And what else could we have done except howl?
There was nothing else

and it burned black.


*Dyfan Lewis*

(Translated by the author)

# Leisure

*(After W.H. Davies)*

Up here, cars call and leave
like fed birds, engines chorusing,
waiting for dusk or deal;
for text, touch,
the cloud-cleared Twmp, or tongue
to run along a paper edge,
a cupped spark,
the green musk of hills.

Days that have been...
diesel, salt and vinegar
trade winds, licking this ridge,
its contusions of height and tide;
Victorian toilets (selling flat whites now)
and on November 5th, this whole wide sky
a smoky, disobedient display.

So stop and stand or sit a while
(don't stare too long)
another grateful captive
of this view. Let the M4 crawl.
See the tramping ramblers,
the phantom tracks of sleds.
Mark the memorial benches,
where the city's dogs
lay their own bouquets.

*Laura Wainwright*

Twmp / mound

# Notes for an Ecologist

It is the Earth itself that is the treasure, not
what is buried in her—the shining hoards of
carbon that feed the rolling mills of the dragon.

We had a life once marked out by the rising
and the setting of the Sun, and by darkness,
with bright Moon and dark Moon, dark cloud or stars.

To the Earth we cleaved for love and for shelter,
her stones were our hearth stones, her trees made our fires
and we cleaved the earth for a giving of seed.

Our implements bit deep into clay and marl, into
shales that resisted the shares of wood and bone
but were shattered and ground by iron and gritstone.

Our fires then were the fires of the Sun, furnaces
blazing in the heat of the day, cold blades we made
that would pierce shale and bone: steel to carry a life away.

We mined ore from the rocks, cut stone for our walls,
dug pigments for staining. Some gave blood in recompense,
others gathered wealth from wasted lives.

We painted our world with the mind's brush
and shaped a story with sharp quills of thought,
sat back satisfied as bright day faded to night.

We viewed it all then in imagination's starlight
waiting for dawn to bring it alive. Dawn comes
gun barrel grey over the subdued land. We grieve.

For the knot that was tied is broken forever
though we try with gestures to the way of right-living
to be something more than brave green consumers.

We find time to mourn for the forest peoples
who prayed to Faunus before their lands were taken,
for the scattered tribes who dwindle in cities.

We have a creed now: to love the Earth,
be carbon neutral, protect the climate.
Will this bring expiation, this guilty posturing?

What of those who profit from the crimes
that revenge themselves on our children,
who impose even death vicariously?

There is no refuge, nor any sanctuary.


*Greg Hill*

**our earth mother is a tough old bitch**

but

*remember*

this is not war

this is merely a struggle with nature
of one species who share this planet
a species that in the year 2020 has
shown its unique capacity for compassion

*do not lose that compassion*

what have we learned from nature's
smallest organism?
it has no care for
the imagined boundaries of race or gender
or nation state

*do not lose that compassion*

our so-called leaders send
mixed message that divide in
the name of unity

one person may interpret that
message in a different way to you        this is their intent

they fear we may unlearn their values
        that personal wealth surpasses global health

           *show tolerance*

           *show understanding*

        remember to share that compassion
        beyond any border / judgementalism they will forge into nationalism /
petty minded parochialism into
        xenophobia /ordinary people elevated
to pedestal for jingoistic rhetoric

        heroes

           hidden enemy

                front line

                    battles ...

           this is the vocabulary of hatred

        *remember* this is not war

war is an invention of
humankind a decision by those
leaders to encourage
           one person     to kill another


*Dominic Williams*

# Dead Mind Running

Beyond tower blocks and estates
of scrutiny and initiation,
young lads run off life's hard lines
in street cages or on any strip of grass
the break in homes provides.
Sprinting after a kicked ball
saves teenagers like religion.

I take my nephews out
and with a few local kids
we play. Football. Always football.

Hope is the ultimate escapism,
and what gives you hope
more than the back of the net,
or the brick wall lining
a neighbour's garden?
It begins to drizzle, and still the boys run.

Each time they score, the local kids
scream at the top of their lungs.
And my nephews join in
until the street is filled
with the demons of stress and discouragement
cast out into the thickening rain.
And then, again, we play.


*Carl Griffin*

## Together, Stronger

*Late June. A restless old seagull is observing 'The Alliance', a leaning hoop balanced on a stainless-steel arrow in front of the Cardiff Central Library. The installation is temporarily draped in red with the words 'Together, Stronger'. In France, the Wales football team is lighting up Euro 2016.*

Nothing clings. Brushed
metal sheds rain,
concrete mildews
the sun-crumbled earth.

What if an arrow fell
in a mighty gust, West Bute
smearing the National Museum
gut, Wagamama crushed

Carluccio carpaccio
Cath Kidston split-open
David Lloyd George twisting
fandango, statuesque John

Batchelor trampling The Hayes
Wahaca dismantling bricks
and mortar? If like them
I splatter in plain sight

of red-brick Wellington
spit-harden gum, my blood
treacle the library wall
for the winding rain

in far Briton Ferry, sunsets
shall crush the hawthorn
clouds on a Sunday stroll
shall hurtle past St. David

a robin would preen
Giant's Grave Road
hear footsteps pacing
the valley, Port Talbot

colluding with old Brunel
in steel. A sudden gust
a gasp, crowd-roar
straw curdled fields

bale and bitter sorrow. In
Mill Lane, brushed metal
gleams one June afternoon
tied to the banner

Together, Stronger
fluttering above
the fireball dancer
sweet first kiss

of skating teens
kids hurling
an oval ball, youth
in relentless crawl.

Honeysuckle scents
an Old Library, the dead
read tales from Mabinogi
I, an old gull

watch a ring lean
whatever brings tomorrow.
France: turns three
then scores, Robson-Kanu.


*Taz Rahman*

## Robson-Kanu

When doubts darken horizons,
when reason is pushed aside for passion,
when old friends turn on each other
and the body politic turns on itself,
growling and frothing like a cur...

I will stop and close my eyes and breathe.
I will stop, close my eyes and remember
Robson-Kanu, and the way he foiled,
Down-field, those three ace defenders,
maintained his poise, held his balance.
How, beset on all sides, he twisted,
turned and flicked his foot, kicking
the most beautiful, unlikely goal
you've ever seen, the ball spinning
past the keeper into the corner of the net.

Robson-Kanu, free agent, unsigned
and not native to this place!
I will remember how a moment of grace
can erase borders, conflicts, rivalries,
as all are caught for precious seconds
in joy, in the wonder it is to be human,
to be Robson-Kanu, to defy chance
in the rain, to be a team not a tribe,
to champion excellence
in the cauldron of the stadium
as the crowd shouts and rises.


*Amy Wack*

## We are a proud nation of call centres,

up-sellers,
begetting zero-hour contracts and failing furloughs.
Onscreen analytics become
new currency of
secrets.

Penned like chickens
some workers use pay like pin money;
preen their urban feathers with
plastic turf
plastic flowers paid with
plastic: the
dead currency
profiting only debt.

Buying in to pay it off
others extend shifts and cover to
cover basic essentials;
find relief in Facebook rants
glorifying the loudest silencer with
crowns of emojis—
cancel culture
cancelling voices.

This hot-desking-not-desking-
Zooming -from-home world,
this tied-to-kitchen-table work
suffocates light.
Blinds for the blinds abound
insulated by factory tinted windows.

Our glass boxes blacken at nightfall
and Kilvey Hill
burns again.

*Anne Phillips*

## Not the Streets

Summer's negative horizons pestering,
dead trees not lasting, still leaves betraying their roots.
Hurricanes and blurred visions,
like birds flying zigzag then landing on their narrow perch.
One can monitor the winds from here.
Step by step they marched, singing nursery rhymes.
Flags and effigies they erected, swinging in the directions of the winds.

These are not the streets I used to know.
Animals wash their bodies in fermented seeds, leftovers, men dancing
with empty bottles of liquor, a lone bee buzzes, sucking nectar from
nearby hibiscus, haggard its
breathing, dying with each stride, it falls. Red lightning strikes,
September rain pours, the king's whip rips.

These are not the streets I used to know.

Brown dark his hairline,
preachers come and go,
marchers of gaiety,
lamentations from a piper's whistle.
In the village of Umuofia Okonkwo fought a good fight.
These winds brought quarrels, a curse amongst us hybrids.

These are not the streets of my youth.


*Eric Ngalle Charles*

# Keeping

*'You promised me a thing that is not possible,*
*that you would give me gloves of the skin of a fish.'*

—Donal Og

There's a woman from Porthcawl
keeping the promise,
making handbags from salmon-skin
cast-offs for Paris
sea-leather renewable.
                            There's Fern creating
androgynous T shirts for LGBT
+ Pride to counter the transgender
suicide rate.
There's Rosie recycling barista coffee
into body polish, cups and candles
with profits for The Wallich homeless.

Out of the middens, the spoil grounds
and landfill, underwater shrubberies
ferns, morays and roses seething,
mamau, chwiorydd a merched
rising between
the lion and the unicorn.

*David Annwn Jones*

# Nightfall

Light cools
  on the hill above the villages.
The shadow line
    is flowing up the field.
See the wounded
  limping from the ridges
with rags tied
    round the remnant of a world.
They watch
  the houses' gradual effacement
under the shadow
    as each light goes out.
The villagers
  are shuttering the casements
and call
    for barricades across the street.

In cities
  in each bright glass-fronted tower
the chief beast squats
    adorned with human love
proclaiming
  that the sorrows will be fewer
if we close up
    the gates and so disprove
the wounded
    who yet march towards the threshold
with burning rags
    to set alight the world.


*Christopher Meredith*

## Fridays for Future
*(After hearing an XR speaker at a Resurgence Conference)*

This is not reported pain.
Distilled softly into lovely words.
Not anodyne and qualified or paled by relativity.
Not triangulated for a shapely truth.
It is the opening of a wound in the speaker.
She's crying as her children come to mind.
I beg you to do something.
She stops just to breathe and continues with resolve
To tell us what led to her conviction.
Lying in the road beneath Parliament.
Watching helicopters roaring above
Avoiding spit and hatred flung from passers by
Glued to her compatriots she had wet her pants.
Shifting in our seats.
We're stunned.
Embarrassed.
Punctured by her truths.
The academic balance is out of kilter.
That's not necessary now that we
can hear her heart beating.
We don't even clap.


*Heather Pudner*

## Pontypool Ski Slope

A summer evening.
Three boys leaning
on bicycles
watched other boys
learn slalom skills.
Each of the three
had a muddy line
like a tyre track
the length of his spine
and a bored look.
They hardly spoke
careful to show
they didn't care.
The laughs and cheers
came from the skiers
boasting of futures
on loftier slopes.
They knew the ropes.
I saw the three
again later
on a bench beside
the shell grotto
blowing smoke rings
across the valley.
If they squinted
they might have seen
the shaft head frame
of the Big Pit
its rigs and jibs
orange and red
in the last of the light.
But they were taken
with horsing around

digs in the ribs
and near the end
of my own descent
to Afon Lwyd
I stepped aside
as they pitched past
at breakneck speed
between the trees
and over a ridge
where their wheels
left the ground.


*Stephen Payne*

## 'Continue watching'

Mae'r nosweithiau'n gwibio heibio
fel rhifynnau cyfresi Netflix,
a does dim yn haws na disgwyl
i'r Drefn ein clymu
i'r rhifyn nesa'
yn y *credits* agoriadol.

Noson ar ôl noson,
rhifyn ar ôl rhifyn,
hyd nes bod box-sets y blynyddoedd
yn pentyrru'n rhesi,

cyn inni sylweddoli na allwn
wylio eto o'r cychwyn.

Weithiau mae gwrthryfela
mor syml
â diffodd y teledu
cyn i'r rhifyn nesa' gydio,

a chanfod eto be alli di wneud
gydag amser.


*Hywel Griffiths*

## 'Continue watching'

The nights fly by
like Netflix series episodes,
and it's so easy to wait
for the System
to bind us
with the next opening credits.

Night after night,
episode by episode,
until our box-set years
are stacked in rows,

before we realise
watching from the beginning
won't play.

Sometimes, uprisings start simply,
by switching the TV off
and rising up off the sofa
before the next episode takes hold,

and discovering the potential
of time.

*Hywel Griffiths*

(Translated by the author)

## in this valley

in this valley we're all immigrants
in this valley
we feel homesick
for our childhood

we feel the burden
of our parents' history
that part that was violent
that part that was uncertain
and that part that was
of hope and longing
and the need to arrive

we forget about hunger
our neighbour does not
laugh at our lack of shoes
our neighbour does not laugh
at our lack of words in
this strange new language

maybe our grand children
will be accepted or maybe
our grandchildren will
despise people who have
endured hardship to be here


*gerhard kress*

## Angin Abowt

ees up there
makin the roof
"more betterer" (ee laughs)
I'm down ere
catchin raindrops
gobbin on earwigs
watchin em curl up
that ole cement bucket
risin on the orange rope
to im up there
doin I doan know what
the flashin on the chimney
nailin the odd slate on
searchin for the screwdriver
what ee's been sat on an then
avin to go back up
the moved ladder to get it

sat on the wall
under the tree
backs to the hedge
well out of the rain
ee passes me a Welsh mint
as the late lunches
come out of The Beverley
the pavement all dug up
traffic jammin
that lorry flattenin those bollards
we laugh at the navvies
swearin at the clerks
behind their thin backs
especially one dozy lookin git
in a yellow plastic mac

"ees a university tyke
knows bugger all about it I'll bet
tryin to teach em their job, christ!
dey knows more than ee'll ever know"
"aye" I replies, lookin at
that sore dark spot
where I jammed my thumb
between two sections of gutterin
to rediscover the agony
an the racism
of a 'black man's pinch'

ee gets up to go back on top
it's not really rainin now
an my thumb's stopped throbbin
ee looks at me, smiles
"university!
dat's where dey
takes yuh brains out yur ead
an shoves em up yur arse init?"


*Tôpher Mills*

## In Other News

While you looked the other way, at
shiny shoes and pristine clothes, another
species died. Another name
wiped from the slate. But it doesn't matter. Your
shiny shoes and pristine clothes and takeaways
are safe, untouched. In other news,
another storm hit another city, but
 it wasn't yours, and another degree
in the earth's temperature is only a degree. After all
you still have shiny shoes and pristine clothes and takeaways and
the mirrored screen of your brand-new phone means
 you don't even need to strain your neck looking
the other way. So keep your eyes
 down as you pass the man with no
shoes and his unfed children, but
watch you're not tripped
by the fragile roots of dying trees.
When you look the other way it's too easy to miss
what hits you.


*Karen Ankers*

# I'm here, while you go
(*after Tagore*)

The sun rises with silver streaks over the bowing cherry tree
and I'm able to send you an image across the world.
I imagine the plum, so dense and sweet under your teeth.
What will you do with the stone? With all of them?
The painted lady and tortoiseshells wash their hands of it,
climbing over the buddleia, combing for sugar.
Sweetness in the hum of the neighbour's saw, too.
The fixation on rebuilding. Clearing his brow before the hammer.

Marigolds throw their faces up to the heat.
I've sent a video congratulating you on your new citizenship,
as a minuscule spider prickles over the skin on my arm.
No money coming, only love;
irrepressible, indestructible, like the ferns sporing once more in the borders
knowing this is not a garden, it drinks like a rainforest.
I've heard the birds in your country, no less miraculous,
singing, 'We are the lucky ones.' Delighted, they are still free to presume.

The saw whines, against a closer grain.
The spider has traversed to the other shoulder.
The sun is getting stronger over the valley's jet-route perimeter
and when it's gently moved, it releases a trapeze wire I can't see
but is clearly there, given how the body swings to safety.
Water uses its influence here, in floodplains and old mine workings,
scours your mouth out, if tempted, as a child, to shout it's not fair.
Let it run, and fill a pixellating harbour with messages. Go.
Keep building bridges.


*Suzanne Iuppa*

## A Resolution

He wrote with the Devil's hand,
so he was strapped for writing.

Imagine the joy of forming a letter,
a G, on a page,
so slowly,
with your own left hand,
the curls in it;

imagine, years later
and in jail.


When writing was the Devil's hand,
speech was the Devil's tongue—
if used against a priest that is.

He wanted to tell his dad,
but his dad was scared of his mother,
and his mother was nearly always drunk
and in hock to the priest,

who, passing by the fireplace,
would make a sign of the cross
ending with an eye-to-eye
and his finger softly
pressed to his lips:
*It's our little secret...*


Imagine being able now
to use that hand to form a letter,
then, making it through the tears,

to write the whole story
you've never been able to write.


*Graham Hartill*

# Author Biographies

**Michael Arnold Williams**. Newport born. His family were founders of their local Labour Party in 1919. With a Baptist chapel background, they were socially active, and he was raised as of the Left. He went to school in Pontypool. Leaving for London he was shocked by the conservatism of the students. As a teacher in H.E. he tried always to empower individuals, irrespective of age, race or gender.

**Malcolm Llywelyn**. 'Bachgen bach o Ferthyr erioed, erioed.' Malcolm is proud of his heritage, language, and culture, and is inspired by the radical history of his hometown of Merthyr Tydfil. He has published books and articles on its historical characters and places. The ancient kingdom of Brycheiniog is now his adopted home and the Welsh language, reflected in its many wonderful place-names, has been the subject of further publications.

**Mike Jenkins**. A Welsh socialist republican activist from Merthyr Tydfil, previously in Cymru Goch and the Welsh Socialist Alliance. Last year Culture Matters published his book of poems in Merthyr dialect *Anonymous Bosch*, with photos by Dave Lewis. His latest book is *Seams of People* (Carreg Gwalch).

**Jacqueline Jones**. Born in West Wales. She is a strong supporter of the NHS. She is a member of the Welsh Group of Artists and the Stuckist Art Movement, a radical grassroots movement. She has been a DJ and has had her music broadcast on the BBC. She has no faith in current political leaders, feeling that none are currently up to the job.

**Phil Knight**. A member of the Socialist Workers Party. He became politically active in his early teens during the 1980s as a member of CND. He has opposed every war fought by both Labour and Conservative governments of the disunited kingdom since then. He is a supporter of an independent Wales, as the break-up of the British state will help to inspire all progressive causes throughout the world. He is a poet who often uses humour to help make a point, as he finds people are more likely to listen to you if you make them laugh, rather than lecturing them about how idiotic they are, because they dare to breathe and disagree with you at the same time.

**Julian Brasington**. A printmaker and writing mentor. An active trade unionist, he has held branch officer roles with UCU and NALGO. His poems have appeared in the *Morning Star*, and in such magazines as *Stand, Ink Sweat & Tears*, and *Channel*. He lives near Conwy and blogs at julianbrasington .com

**Patrick Dobbs**. Nine years itinerant agricultural worker. Over sixty years hill farmer on Brecon Beacons in East Carmarthenshire. His latest book *Tales from a Mountain Farm* (Cowry Publishing) tells of a farming life in fifty verses.

**Simone Mansell Broome**. Tenby-born, and back in Wales since 2007. Loves both spoken and written word. Wit. Etymology. Believes in freedom of speech, fairness, tolerance and inclusivity. Deeply concerned about the environment. Veggie for four decades; now vegan. Wishes her new passport was red, not black. Hates cliques, cronyism and corruption. Descended from farmers, peasants, artisans, self-made men, suffragists and Gunpowder plotters.

**Huw Pudner**. A retired primary school teacher, and lives in Ynysmeudwy in the Swansea Valley. He writes songs in the folk tradition, and poetry. Many of his songs are about life in Wales. He is closely involved with the Valley Folk Club. He is an active socialist and has been involved in several anti-war, environmental and housing campaigns. He believes that the mass activity of working-class men and women is a key ingredient for the revolutionary transformation of society... climate chaos, the fight against racism and the far right, and the struggle to improve workers' rights, are just a few of the battlefields where we need to see our side making big gains.

**Des Mannay**. A Welsh writer of colour, and part of the Punk generation, who opposed the Nazi NF. A long-time community activist, former shop steward in NALGO and GMB. Had articles published in *Socialist Worker, Socialist Review*, and *Planet Magazine*. Was on the Editorial Board of *Welsh Socialist Voice*. First poetry collection, *Sod 'em—and tomorrow*, published by Waterloo Press.

**Menna Elfyn**. Award-winning poet and playwright, who has published fourteen collections of poetry, mainly with Bloodaxe Books. Her forthcoming collection in Welsh, *Tosturi/Mercy* (Barddas), will be published in March 2022. Through her work and activism, she has been translated into 20 languages, and two new books in Swedish and Spanish will appear in 2022. She is President of Wales PEN Cymru, and Emeritus Professor at University of Wales, Trinity Saint David.

**Sheenagh Pugh**. Spent most of her life in Wales writing political stuff, but trying not to be too obvious about it. She now lives in Shetland, has turned to ecological concerns and thinks it might be better if humans made themselves extinct before they do it to all other species. Her current collection is *Afternoons Go Nowhere* (Seren Books, 2019), from which this poem comes.

**J. Brookes**. Born SE London in 1951. Had a tramping sort of youth. Went to the New University of Ulster. Taught in Sudan and Turkey. Moved to Cardiff in 1992. Ran *Yellow Crane* poetry mag. *Selected Poems* published by Parthian Books in 2019.

**Xavier Panadès I Blas**. 'The Catalan', has been instrumental in the internationalisation of Catalan culture. For the last two decades, he has stunned audiences around the world with his explosive performances in Catalan. Readers are typically captivated by his reflective stories and poems, which encourage people to take ownership of the socio-environmental problem looming over humanity.

**Tim Evans**. Poet and activist born in Llanelli. He was taught by Raymond Williams, his tutor at Cambridge University. He worked as a teacher and lecturer and was active in the National Union of Teachers (now the NEU) and the National Association of Teachers in Further and Higher Education (now the UCU). He organises the Llanelli 1911 Rail Strike Commemoration which annually marks the shooting of protestors in Llanelli by Churchill's troops. He co-runs Live Poets Society, a political poetry group based in Swansea. His work has been published by Parthian, and has appeared in *Planet, New Welsh Review* and the *International Socialism Journal* (ISJ). His article on Welsh Syndicalism and the Cambrian Combine Strike was published in the *ISJ* in 2021. His latest poetry collection, *Bones of the Apocalypse* was also published by Frequency House in 2021.

**Rhoda Thomas**. Co-founder of the Swansea-based Live Poets Society, Red Poet and a fellow coordinator of events such as Llanelli 1911 and Calon Lân, Rhoda regularly contributes to live and online events, particularly in relation to violence against women and anti-racism. In 2021, her work was included in the Nashville-based Poetry in the Brew anthology *Sinew* and in *Seventh Quarry* magazine, and is to be found in *Onward/Ymlaen!* and *Land of Change*, as well as in her latest solo collection *Imago*.

**Myrddin ap Dafydd**. Fel cyhoeddwyr llyfrau, mae gan Wasg Carreg Gwalch gyfrifoldeb i rannu gwybodaeth a syniadau. Mae hanes a threftadaeth—meysydd sy'n cyfrannu'n helaeth at hunaniaeth Cymru—yn amlwg yn y rhan fwyaf o'n cyhoeddiadau. Bu'n bryder mawr nad oedd deunydd o'r fath ar gael ar gyfer plant Cymry ond gobeithio bod pethau'n well erbyn hyn. Mae digon o waith 'w wneud o hyd, ac i bontio hefyd rhwng Cymru a gwledydd a diwylliannau eraill.

**Myrddin ap Dafydd**. Runs Carreg Gwalch Press, which has a responsibility to share information and ideas, history and heritage—areas that make a major contribution to Welsh identity—and which feature prominently in most of their publications. It has been a great worry that such material is not available for Welsh children but hopefully things are better now. There is still plenty of work to be done, and also a bridge between Wales and other countries and cultures.

**Anna Powell**. A deaf poet, Anna's nature writing explores sensory extension. After retiring as Critical Theory Reader (Literature, Film) at Manchester Met, she returned to Ynys Môn where she helps organise community arts events and attends the Poetry School. Anna has two poems in *Lucent Dreaming*, where she won Third Prize in 2021. She's currently writing on ecological issues for activist groups.

**Annest Gwilym**. The author of two books of poetry: *Surfacing* (2018) and *What the Owl Taught Me* (2020), both published by Lapwing Poetry. Annest has been published in numerous literary journals and anthologies, both online and in print, and placed in several writing competitions, winning one. She is a nominee for Best of the Net 2021. Twitter: @AnnestGwilym.

**Peter Finch**. Has been writing poetry since the 1960s. His *Collected Poems* appears from Seren Books this year. He was convinced when he began writing that something was not right with how society worked. Fifty years later he believes that is still the case. He continues to write.

**Kathy Miles**. A poet and short story writer living in West Wales. Her poetry has appeared widely in magazines and anthologies, and her fourth full collection, *Bone House*, was published by Indigo Dreams in 2020. She was born in Liverpool, and after moving to Wales, became acutely aware of the part Liverpool played in the flooding of Capel Celyn. She often passes the 'Cofiwch Dryweryn' sign; each time, she feels the weight of shame.

**Mae Mererid Hopwood**. Wedi treulio ei gyrfa yn astudio a dysgu ieithoedd a llenyddiaeth. Enillodd Gadair, Coron a Medal Ryddiaith yr Eisteddfod Genedlaethol a bu'n fardd plant Cymru. Bu'n Gadeirydd Cymdeithas y Cymod ond gadawodd y rôl honno er mwyn darparu ysgrifenyddiaeth i Academi Heddwch Cymru.

**Mererid Hopwood**. Has spent her career studying and teaching languages and literature. She won the Chair and Crown for poetry and the Prose Medal at the National Eisteddfod, and has been Children's Laureate for Wales. She left her role as Chair of Cymdeithas y Cymod (International Fellowship of Reconciliation, Wales) to provide secretariat for Academi Heddwch, (the Wales Peace Institute).

**Rachel Carney**. Is a PhD student and creative writing tutor based in Cardiff. Her poems, reviews and articles have been published in several magazines including *Poetry Wales, Anthropocene, Ink Sweat & Tears* and *Acumen.* Her poem 'Understood' came second in the Bangor Poetry Competition in 2021. Two of her poems have been shortlisted for the Bridport Prize. She blogs at https://createdtoread.com. 'Yellow' was originally published on the Cynon Valley Museum website as part of a residency in June 2020, responding to works of art produced by local Welsh artists. It refers to the canaries used in coal mines.

**Ifor ap Glyn**. Bardd Cenedlaethol Cymru ers 2016—ac yn cefnogi annibyniaeth i Gymru ers tipyn cyn hynny.

**Ifor ap Glyn**. National Poet of Wales since 2016—and a supporter of Welsh independence since a while before that.

**Brian Thomas Phillips**. Born in the 50s into a post-industrial graveyard in Swansea. He thought his homeland had been devastated by aliens and wasn't far wrong. Industrialists always inhabit a different world; one bereft of conscience, empathy and environmental concern. He is far to the left of Jeremy Corbyn. The one topic more urgent than socio-political justice is environmental husbandry. His poetry and lyrics reflect this.

**Alun Rees**. Born 1937, Heolgerrig, Merthyr Tydfil. Journalist all working life. Former Welsh Sports Writer of the Year and winner of Harri Webb award. Bit old and doddery for much activism these days. Core belief a truly independent Wales with a seat at the UN. Most recent publication: *Ballad of the Black Domain* (Culture Matters, 2021).

**Jeremy Hooker**. Published many books of poetry, literary criticism, and diaries; the most recent book being *The Release*, Shearsman, 2022, which received the Poetry Book Society Wild Card prize. He is an emeritus professor of the University of South Wales and a Fellow of the Royal Society of Literature, and of the Learned Society of Wales. He lives in retirement in Treharris.

**Jason Glover**. Teacher, administrator, 53. In love with Cerys and father of Nye and Bill, who are weaving their way through their 20's. Writes on trains. Describes the inside of an instance.

**Gae Stenson**. Was a late literary bloomer. She gained an English degree in her thirties and Masters in Creative Writing in her fifties. Active in disability rights in the 1970s, later in life, she served as disability officer on her local Labour CLP. The focus of her writing is on the outsiders in society. At present, she is working on her first novel. Gae is also an occasional blogger where she shares first drafts of her poems, short stories, and novels: https://gestensonwriting.wordpress.com

**Eric Morgan**. Left school at sixteen and after a number of jobs graduated from Coleg Harlech. He has been active in the Trade Union all his life and has never let his membership lapse, and is still a member though now retired. Following damage to his spinal cord he is now wheelchair-bound and lives in supported accommodation.

**Phil Coleman.** Has been protesting for the past forty years—against nuclear weapons, against student hall rent hikes, against the climate catastrophe, against Iraq, against Brexit, against Thatcher, against Blair, against Boris, against the occupation of Tibet, against animal exploitation, against global debt and apartheid. But he's always believed a better world, and a better way of living in it and with each other, is possible.

**Steve Griffiths**. Born in Ynys Môn, was a researcher, policymaker and campaigner on social and health inequality, including work on reducing hospital admissions. Now he is preoccupied with democracy. Poetry from seven previous collections, all but the first published in Wales, is gathered in *Weathereye: Selected Poems* (2019). He appears to have run out of publishers. His website is www.stevegriffithspoet.com. A version of 'The One Percent' appeared on the **Culture Matters** website.

**Sally Spedding**. A twin, who was born and brought up on those wild sand dunes in Newton near Porthcawl. The sudden move to grey, overcrowded, suburban London, then Manchester, where her Dutch-born father held a senior post with Unilever, was a shock which became, it seemed, her perpetual shadow. A longing for space and wild nature was why Coed-y-Twyn set high on the Blorenge mountain near Abergavenny, became so special. When Jeffrey, her artist husband, finally retired from Northampton University, they headed back to West Wales, where the River Loughor courses down to the sea from the Black Mountain alongside their large garden, and the fearless friendship of so many different birds is ever-present... paradise.

**Rob Cullen**. Grew up in the Rhondda, and trained as an artist, art teacher, and social worker. Rob has worked in a steel works, on construction sites, the railways, in psychiatric hospitals, and for social services and Barnardos. Rob worked for forty years with working-class kids, who were damaged and damaging, who when they grew up, were even more damaged and damaging. Rob was a committee member of a housing association, providing housing for women who'd suffered from domestic violence. He's been a union member in every job he's held. Education is being destroyed and kids are being left on the rubbish heap at a young age—so what's changed since he was a kid in the 1950s?

**Ric Hool**. The author of 11 collections of poetry and has run the reading series Poetry Upstairs for 33 years. His most recent publication, *Containing Multitudes* (2022), is a collaboration with Artist Tim Rossiter and includes a Welsh translation by Frank Olding. *Since I last Wrote* will be published in 2023 by Red Squirrel Press. Ric Hool is from Northumberland, but lives in Wales.

**David Lloyd**. Is the author of three poetry collections (*Warriors, The Gospel According to Frank*, and *The Everyday Apocalypse*); and three works of fiction (*Boys: Stories and a Novella, Over the Line*, and *The Moving of the Water*). He directs the Creative Writing Program at Le Moyne College in Syracuse, New York, USA. 'Sitting Bull' originally appeared in *Warriors* ( Salt, 2012)

**John Williams**. Has taken part in vital protests from environmental, republican, poll tax, criminal justice bill, LGBTQ Rights, RAR, Anarchist festivals, Anti-police brutality, Reclaim the streets Merthyr Rising, etc. He has exhibited and constructed art installations for independence, showing exploitation and corruption by local puppets working for Westminster.

**Harry Rogers**. Socialist and activist from Ceredigion in West Wales, Harry Rogers has written poetry, song lyrics, and short stories since the 1970's. Currently working on new songs with his band Scene Red and a new collection of poems called *Cwtch Me In The Now* to be published in February 2022.

**Peter Jones** is a retired teacher who writes short stories and poetry, and has performed in varied venues including heritage railways, community arts centres, pubs, libraries, theatres, cafés and village halls. He is a member of Chester Poets, Pinboard Writers, and Hawarden Ink, Hope Community Library Creative Writing Group and the newly formed Caffi Isa Writers' Group. He has taken part in Wrexham's Carnival of Words on a number of occasions and one of his short stories, Twm Golau, won second prize. He's also been shortlisted for the Robert Graves Poetry Prize. Peter was a chapter author in the academic work, *The Principal—Power and Professionalism in FE* (UCL 2017), and his latest collection, *Tears Flow*, was published in March 2022.

**Mae Aneirin Karadog**. Yn fardd, ieithydd a darlledwr sy'n byw gyda'i deulu ym Mhontyberem. Gyda gwreiddiau yn Ne Cymru ddiwydianol ac yn Llydaw amaethyddol, a magwraeth lle y'i magwyd trwy gyfrwng y Gymraeg a'r Llydaweg, mae achos ieithoedd lleiafrifol fel Cymraeg a Llydaweg yn agos at ei galon ac annibyniaeth i wledydd fel Cymru a Llydaw hefyd yn bwysig iddo.

**Aneirin Karadog**. A poet, linguist and broadcaster, living in Pontyberem with his family. He has roots in industrial South Wales and in agricultural Brittany, an upbringing through the medium of Welsh and Breton, and so the cause of minority languages is close to his heart, as is the struggle for independence of countries such as Wales and Brittany. Thanks to the publisher Barddas for permission to use the Welsh language version of 'Aberfan and Pontyberem'.

**Peter Thabit Jones**. Welsh poet and dramatist, has authored fourteen books. He has participated in festivals and conferences in America and Europe and is an annual writer-in-residence in Big Sur, California. A recipient of many awards, including the Eric Gregory Award for Poetry (the Society of Authors, London) and the Homer: European Medal of Poetry and Art, two of his dramas for the stage have premiered in America and the UK. His opera libretti for Luxembourg composer Albena Petrovic-Vratchanska have premiered at the Philharmonie Luxembourg, the National Opera House Stara Zagora, and the Theatre National Du Luxembourg. He is the founder and editor of The Seventh Quarry Press and *The Seventh Quarry* magazine. www.peterthabitjones.com

**M.S. Evans**. A Pushcart nominated poet and photographer residing in Butte, Montana. A descendant of Welsh and Polish emigrants, Evans is committed to promoting working-class solidarity and internationalism. Twitter: @ SeaNettleInk. Instagram: @seanettleart

**Ness Owen**. A poet and FE lecturer from Ynys Môn, who works in the community. She is an avid supporter of the community voice and protecting the right to peaceful protest. She is a member of UCU and Yes Cymru and has marched for Indy Cymru, Nid yw Cymru ar Werth, Cymru in Europe, Save Penrhos and protecting our NHS.

**Jackie Biggs**. A former news journalist and editor, who writes poetry with a political and social comment stance that is often extensively researched. Much of her recent work addresses the climate crisis. Her political poetry has been published by *I am not a silent poet* and *Poetry24* online, as well as in the annual magazine *Red Poets*. She performs her poetry at events and festivals in West Wales, where she lives.

**Samantha Mansi**. Studying for a Masters in Creative Writing and is a passionate left-wing feminist and activist. She took part in Llanelli uprising 1918 pre-Covid, and live poets. She looks forward to publishing her political poetry in the future.

**Rosy Wood-Bevan**. A life-long, sporadic poet, Rosy enjoys performing at local poetry nights such as Talisman, Live Poets and People Speak Up. Published in *Seventh Quarry* magazine and a previous edition of *Red Poets*, her themes are often more intimate than outwardly political, reflecting her interest, as a psychotherapist, in people, relationships, emotions and family history.

**Caroline Richards**. Found herself sitting at a formica table in a village in Northern Thailand in 2018, freewriting for the first time in a class led by the queer Irish activist, poet, Cat Brogan. Since then her drive to write and deliver has remained constant, as a way of processing feelings and events. Aside from contributing to Cardiff's spoken word scene, Caroline enjoys a varied career, encompassing visual arts, carnival and circus. Surreal achievements so far include an experience akin to *The Magus* whilst preparing a performance of *Merlin* to a stadium of 20,000 in remote central China; teaching biology to wonderfully characterful Cambodian grade 5 students; becoming a consultant tutor at a prestigious Art and Design Academy in Southern China; and possibly trickiest of all... succeeding in riding the unicycle. All were glorious but unplanned and that is why she trusts fate with the reins; fate, creativity and organic muesli.

**Dave Rendle**. A poet from Cardigan who hates Tories and fascists and is committed to the causes of freedom, peace, human rights and the creation of an independent Welsh Socialist Republic. A member of local poetry group The Cellar Bards, he is also a keen blogger under the name *teifidancer*.

**Mike Douse**. Has worked in international education since 1964, having been a teacher in Liverpool and Sydney, a head teacher in Cardiff and Nigeria, a university professor in Ghana, the foundation director of Australia's Disadvantaged Schools Programme and, for the last three decades, an advisor to the EU, DfID, Unesco and ILO on educational programmes in developing countries. He has been in peaceful protests in Belfast, Aldermaston, Fiji and London (occupying the South African Embassy) and bears the scars upon his back to prove it. In addition to books, journal articles and conference publications on matters educational, Mike has published three anthologies of poetry: *Old Ground, Gone to Ground and Grounded*.

**Siôn Tomos Owen**. A writer in both English and Welsh, and an illustrator and presenter from Treorchy, Rhondda Fawr. Among the programmes he has presented is the series *Pobol y Rhondda* about people from his own valley. His creative work varies from prose to poetry, illustration to murals, with a focus on socialist history & protest songs. He tweets under @Siônmun

**Rebecca Lowe**. A poet and Quaker peace activist, based in Swansea, UK. An active member of Live Poets, she is also a media volunteer for Swansea City of Sanctuary, where she advocates for the rights of asylum seekers and refugees, many of whom face destitution and discrimination.

**Guinevere Clark**. Poet-researcher, using the lens of matricentric feminism on a Creative Writing PhD at Swansea University. She has formed a 70-poem collection, *The Egg in the Triangle*, which covers the multivalence of motherhood, intersecting with sexuality and place. Her work raises voice around domestic abuse, gender inequality and the liminal spaces within motherhood. She was a commissioned poet on the 2019-2020 touring Dear Christine project, contributing to a feminist re-writing of the life of Christine Keeler, has formed part of a writing group with Swansea Women's Aid, and delivered creative writing workshops for Swansea's Fusion project and Arts Care's The Friday Project. Her first poetry book is *Fresh Fruit and Screams* (2006). Guinevere's poems have been published in: *Magma, A3, Minerva Rising, nawr, Atlanta Review, Black Bough*, and *Blackbox Manifold*, among others, and she was a commended poet in the 2020 Ambit Poetry Competition. Guinevere has advocated the development of creative women's spaces for over 20 years, with dance, visual art, performance, and creative writing and founded a Community Interest Company, receiving generous European Social Funding for her creative project work with women. Visit: www.guinevereclark. com

**Mary Kaye**. Cardiff born, started writing poetry in her teens, mainly for her own purposes and enjoyment. Having worked in mental health (RMN) for over 30 years, she is now focusing on her writing more. She's had a few poems published in magazines such as *Roundhouse* and *Red Poets* and hopes that her poetry will lead to a book someday. Mary's main areas of activism centre on mental health, women's rights and related issues.

**Karen Gemma Brewer**. Born of coal-mining and farm-working stock, is an award-winning poet and performer from Ceredigion, championing equality and environmental issues. She leads initiatives enabling the LGBTQ+ community to tell their own stories and is editor of *Write It OUT—an anthology of new LGBTQ+ writing from Ceredigion & Carmarthenshire*. A second edition of her poetry collection *Seeds From A Dandelion* is out now, and a new collection *Dancing In The Sun* is due soon.

**Tracey Rhys**. A Welsh writer, artist and freelance editor from the South Wales valleys. In 2020, she won the Poetry Archive's WordView competition; a video-reading of which is now available in the permanent archive. Her first collection, *Teaching a Bird to Sing* (Green Bottle, 2016) was the result of a Literature Wales New Writer's Award, which allowed her time to write about her relationship with her young son, who has a diagnosis of Autism Spectrum Disorder. Tracey's poetry on autism has featured in two professional theatre productions with Winterlight Theatre (*Company of Sirens*), and has been exhibited at the Senedd for Autism Awareness month. Tracey has published poetry and essays with *Poetry Wales, Planet: The Welsh Internationalist, New Welsh Review, The Lonely Crowd, Ink Sweat & Tears*, amongst others. She has work in anthologies *Poems from the Borders* (Seren Books), *Bloody Amazing!* (Dragon-Yaffle Press), and is forthcoming in *A470* (Arachne Press), *Land of Change* (Culture Matters). Her first story publication will be in *Welsh Women Writing Crime* (Honno Press), due May 2022. Tracey is a graduate of the MA in Creative Writing at Cardiff University. 'The Mud Service' was first published in *Planet*, written in response to the Hinkley Point / Cardiff Bay nuclear mud-dumping scandal.

**Adele Cordner**. A writer, performer and director from Newport. She is a feminist and nature-lover. Her recent short play, *The Firestarter*, performed by Dirty Protest for Newport Rising, raised awareness of the astonishing number of murders of women in the past year. Two of her new plays will be performed this year by local companies. Adele's first poetry pamphlet, *The Kitchen Sink Chronicles* was published by Hedgehog Poetry Press in 2021, and her full collection *Tea & Toast* will be published by the same, later this year. Her work is published in magazines and anthologies including *Red Poets* (Mike Jenkins), *Poems for Grenfell Tower* (The Onslaught Press, 2018), *Ways to Peace Anthology* (On the Edge Publishing, 2019), *Pandemic Poetry Anthology* (Yarn Whispering, 2020), and placed in competitions including *Poetry on The Lake*, the Plough Prize and the Welsh Poetry Competition. Adele hosts the Newport Stanza poetry workshop group. Website: https://adelecordner.com. Twitter: @adele_cordner

**Phil Howells**. Retired South Wales journalist. Career included news and sports reporting, production and editing in Merthyr Tydfil, and Cardiff as *South Wales Echo* sub-editor. Freelance work for national and regional newspapers. Contributed to former Merthyr free newspaper. Later worked in Civil Service. Committee member of local organisations.

**Kitty Jay**. A poetic chameleon. Whether through humour, metaphor or experimenting with different bardic forms, Kitty Jay's lyrics aim to provoke a response. Unafraid to get tangled in the complexities of human behaviour, or daring to empathise and understand human frailty, Kitty Jay reminds us of the fallen human condition in a darkening spiritual world.

**Maggie Harris**. Born in Guyana and has lived in Wales and England. She has published six collections of poetry, three short story collections and a memoir, *Kiskadee Girl*. She has worked as Kent Reader Development Worker and International Teaching Fellow at Southampton University. Her work as a writer is concerned with Caribbean history and migration, highlighting the lives and reconnecting the diaspora through her poetry. She has won the Guyana Prize twice for her poetry and the Commonwealth Short Story Prize for her story 'Sending for Chantal'. Last year she was the Winner of the Welsh Poetry Award with her poem 'and the thing is'.

**Gemma June Howell**. A grassroots activist, writer, poet, tutor, academic and Associate Editor for Culture Matters. Founder of the CSOS, she co-organised the Sister March (Cardiff, 2017). She is regularly published in *Red Poets* and performs at the Merthyr Rising Festival. Her work has appeared in Bloodaxe Books (2015), *The London Magazine* (2020), and she was invited to discuss her Anglo-Welsh dialect poetry on *Tongue & Talk* (produced by award-winning Made in Manchester, for BBC Radio 4, 2021). Gemma has recently submitted her PhD—an emancipatory project exploring collective trauma and transcendence. Entitled *Concrete Diamonds*, it's a hybrid novel featuring an interwoven, eco-feminist mythopoeic tale and graffiti concrete poems. Ultimately a polyphonic homage to working-class people living on the margins of post-industrial neoliberal Britain, the work aims to capture the life world of five generations of women, encompassing a range of literary styles from the poetic to polemic, phantasmagorical to academic, gritty realism and dark comedic. Gemma is currently editing the forthcoming Culture Matters anthology, *Land of Change: Stories of Struggle & Solidarity from Wales*. As an exercise in social excavation, the anthology features prose, artwork, and photography, to unearth and showcase the cultural diversity of lived experience in Wales.

**Julian Meek**. Writer, poet, journalist and Christian priest has been a Plaid Cymru supporter since his teenage years and a member for two decades. He supports independence for Wales and a compassionate renegotiation of the relationship between the individual countries of Britain. Is also an LGBTQ rights activist whose book *Entering into the Mystery* was chosen as one of the top 25 'rainbow Christian' books of 2014 by *Jesus in Love*, a leading online resource in America.

**John Freeman.** His *What Possessed Me* (Worple Press), won the Roland Mathias award in 2017. Other recent books include *Strata Smith and the Anthropocene* (KFS Press, 2016), which addresses the environmental crisis. His latest collection is *Plato's Peach* (Worple Press, 2021). His 'Mask of Sanity' is inspired by 'The Mask of Anarchy' of Shelley, on whose radicalism Freeman has written numerous essays. The poem first appeared on the blog page of *Tears in the Fence* (https://tearsinthefence.com/202/06/30/the-mask-of-sanity-by-john-freeman/).

**Mae Dyfan Lewis.** Yn llenor o Craig-cefn-parc. Mae'n ysgrifennu mewn sawl cyfrwng. Sefydlodd Gwasg Pelydr yn 2018, sy'n cyhoeddi gwaith arbrofol gan artisitaid a llenorion.

**Dyfan Lewis.** A writer from Craig-cefn-parc. He writes in a variety of mediums. He founded Gwasg Pelydr in 2018, a platform that publishes experimental work by artists and writers. 'Gelliwastad ar dân' was previously published in the anthology *Stamp* and pamphlet *Mawr*.

**Laura Wainwright** is the author of a poetry pamphlet, *Air and Armour* (Green Bottle Press, 2021) and the literary-critical book *New Territories in Modernism: Anglophone Welsh Writing, 1930- 1949* (University of Wales Press, 2018). She has written non-fiction and poetry for the environmental charity, Sustainable Wales, and currently works for a charity helping people in the city of Newport, South Wales. 'Leisure' was first published in *New Welsh Review/ New Welsh Reader* #125 and was commissioned by Sustainable Wales/Cymru Gynaliadwy for their Our Square Mile/Ein Milltir Sgwar project, now Shared Horizons/Gorwelion.

**Greg Hill** has been a producer, editor, reviewer and commentator on literature in Wales for many years. He also has a history of participating in direct action with CND, Cymdeithas yr Iaith, as well as support for radical politics, environmental issues and campaigns for social justice.

**Dominic Williams** never considered himself an activist poet. Certainly very little of his creative work is overtly political. His protest, if it exists, is the manner in which he employs poetry on a daily basis, to imbue the workshop activities and celebrations of the language arts that he arranges with egalitarianism. His tools of revolution are compassion and respect. Those he opposes are any people who control by fear: governments or scientists, religious leaders or environmentalists; anyone who exploits the faith inherent in humankind, corrupting it into zealotry.

**Carl Griffin** is from Swansea. He is editor of one collaborative poetry book (*Arrival at Elsewhere*) and author of one collection (*Throat of Hawthorn*). His poem 'Dead Mind Running' explores sport as escapism, and the need for housing estates to provide space for youngsters to escape the stress of school, gangs and home life.

**Taz Rahman.** Cardiff-based writer and founder of the YouTube channel Just Another Poet. He has been published in *Poetry Wales, South Bank Poetry* and *Nation Cymru.* He is passionate about making nature more accessible. His photojournalism, documenting political activism in South Wales, has featured in national and international publications.

**Amy Wack.** Born in California. She moved to Wales in 1988. She worked for 30 years for Seren Books as a Poetry Editor, and helped to publish disabled writers like Polly Atkin, and recently a fine translation by Jenny Lewis of the poet Adnan Al Sayegh's noted surrealist epic of his persecution and exile from Iraq, *Let Me Tell You What I Saw.*

**Anne Phillips** believes there are so many things wrong today: welfare cut to the bone; cuts to the NHS and to education; lack of opportunity for youth; cuts to youth services; a mental health crisis. Otherwise she is retired after a life-changing illness and now lives, works and writes bilingually in South Wales.

**Eric Ngalle Charles.** A Cameroonian writer, poet, and playwright based in Wales. He was awarded the Creative Wales Award 2017/2018 for his work on the topics of migration, trauma, and memory. In 'I, Eric Ngalle: One Man's Journey Crossing Continents from Africa to Europe' (2019), he recounts his journey to Wales. He sits on the boards of Literature Wales and Aberystwyth Arts Centre Advisory Group and has been pursuing a PhD at King's College London since October 2021.

**David Annwn Jones** led a successful campaign for the racist poem 'Taffy was a Welshman' to be removed from *The Rattle Bag* anthology (Faber), widely taught in schools. For long an active campaigner against development on green belt land and fracking, his poem 'Farigoule' features in the Extinction Rebellion *Rebel Talk* anthology and his 'Sheard's Quarry' in the eco- 'Magazine': *Extraction on the Edge of an Abyss.*

**Christopher Meredith.** The award-winning author of five novels, a book of short stories and several poetry collections. Latest fiction is the short novel *Please* and latest poetry collection is *Still*, in which 'Nightfall' first appeared, both published by Seren Books in 2021. A lifelong socialist who's dedicated his life and work in both languages to Wales. He was born and brought up in Tredegar and lives in Brecon. 'Nightfall' was first published in *Still* (Seren Books, 2021).

**Heather Pudner**. A woman who writes and sings in between pushing for change, reading, gardening and making things. Convinced of the power of companionship to share the struggles of everyday life and shoulder trouble, she is increasingly aware that objections and action are within everyone's grasp and with persistence will produce results. Retired from a life working in education, she is learning, after years of protesting, that time really is short and we must now raise our voices even louder.

**Stephen Payne** was born in Merthyr Tydfil and lives in Penarth, South Glamorgan. His first full collection, *Pattern Beyond Chance*, was published in 2015 by HappenStance Press and shortlisted for Wales Book of the Year. His second collection, *The Windmill Proof*, was published by the same press in September 2021. 'Pontypool Ski Slope' was previously published in the *New Welsh Reader*.

**Mae Hywel Griffiths**. Yn fardd ac yn ddaearyddwr yn Adran Daearyddiaeth a Gwyddorau Daear, Prifysgol Aberystwyth. Mae ganddo ddiddordeb mawr mewn cydweithio rhwng gwyddonwyr a beirdd er mwyn ysbrydoli pobl i ymwneud â'r argyfwng hinsawdd. Mae'n gweld yr argyfwng hinsawdd yn rhan o argyfwng cyfalafiaeth sy'n bygwth dyfodol y Gymraeg a chymunedau Cymru a chymunedau tebyg ar draws y byd.

**Hywel Griffiths**. A poet and geographer in the Department of Geography and Earth Sciences, Aberystwyth University. He is interested in how collaboration between poets and scientists can engage people in the climate crisis. He sees the climate crisis as part of the crisis of capitalism that threatens the future of the Welsh language and Welsh communities and similar communities across the world.

**gerhard kress** has written children's books where the main character is an ex-miner and compassionate environmentalist, who lives in the woods near Pontypridd. He's been involved in marches and action against the Vietnam War, the fascist dictatorship of Pinochet, and the right- wing press, by blocking the delivery from the printing press. In the 1970s he worked in a therapeutic community for people with learning disabilities and helped build up a business by encouraging the town to recycle waste paper and by organising systematic street collections. In recent years he has supported the renewed campaign against the relentless destruction of the environment for profit. He was at the protest in Merthyr against the rally led by the appalling racist Nigel Farage and used his photographs and observations to produce a book, Immigrants built Merthyr.

**Tôpher Mills**. Born in Cardiff, where he still lives. He has had many poems and stories published in a large variety of places including: *Poetry Wales, New Welsh Review, The North, Scintilla, The Rialto, Orbis, Quadrant*, and broadcast on radio and television, etc. He has written regular columns in *The Western Mail* and *The New Welsh Review*. His *New and Selected Poems: Sex On Toast* is available from Parthian Press.

**Karen Ankers**. A poet, playwright and novelist, who defines as a socialist and who often finds herself politically homeless. Her work is fed by the desire for a world in which all are treated fairly, and in which the planet is loved and respected. Her primary concern is with animal rights and welfare.

**Suzanne Iuppa**. A poet and conservationist working in the Dyfi Valley, mid-Wales. She has coordinated climate resilience projects in Wales for several years. She is inspired by ecology, the farming community where she lives, and day-to-day relationships, with recent work in *And Other Poems, Good Dadhood*, and *Natur Cymru*. She's a columnist for *Spelt* and Writer-in-Residence at Climate.Cymru.

**Graham Hartill** moved to Wales from the industrial Midlands and in the 1980s became a mainstay of the burgeoning poetry scene in Cardiff. He has run countless writing workshops in community settings, especially in mental health settings and with elderly people, and recently retired after 15 years of working as a writer in prisons. He teaches postgraduate students Creative Writing for Therapeutic Purposes for the Metanoia Institute, the only course of its kind in the world. His most recent collection is *Rhapsodies*, published by Aquifer Books in 2021.